OFFICIAL
SQA SPECIMEN
QUESTION PAPER
AND HODDER GIBSON
MODEL QUESTION PAPERS
ANSWERS

NATIONAL 5

MODERN STUDIES

2013 Specimen Question Paper & 2013 Model Papers

HODDER
GIBSON
LEARN MORE

This book contains the official 2013 SQA Specimen Question Paper for National 5 Modern Studies, with associated SQA approved answers modified from the official marking instructions that accompany the paper.

In addition the book contains model practice papers, together with answers, plus study skills advice. These papers, some of which may include a limited number of previously published SQA questions, have been specially commissioned by Hodder Gibson, and have been written by experienced senior teachers and examiners in line with the new National 5 syllabus and assessment outlines, Spring 2013. This is not SQA material but has been devised to provide further practice for National 5 examinations in 2014 and beyond.

Hodder Gibson is grateful to the copyright holders, as credited on the final page of the Answer Section, for permission to use their material. Every effort has been made to trace the copyright holders and to obtain their permission for the use of copyright material. Hodder Gibson will be happy to receive information allowing us to rectify any error or omission in future editions.

Hachette UK's policy is to use papers that are natural, renewable and recyclable products and made from wood grown in sustainable forests. The logging and manufacturing processes are expected to conform to the environmental regulations of the country of origin.

Orders: please contact Bookpoint Ltd, 130 Park Drive, Abingdon, Oxon OX14 4SE. Telephone: (44) 01235 827720. Fax: (44) 01235 400454. Lines are open 9.00–5.00, Monday to Saturday, with a 24-hour message answering service. Visit our website at www.hoddereducation.co.uk. Hodder Gibson can be contacted direct on: Tel: 0141 848 1609; Fax: 0141 889 6315; email: hoddergibson@hodder.co.uk

This collection first published in 2013 by
Hodder Gibson, an imprint of Hodder Education,
An Hachette UK Company
2a Christie Street
Paisley PA1 1NB

₹BrightRED Hodder Gibson is grateful to Bright Red Publishing Ltd for collaborative work in preparation of this book and all SQA Past Paper and National 5 Model Paper titles 2013.

Typeset by PDQ Digital Media Solutions Ltd, Bungay, Suffolk NR35 1BY

Printed in the UK

A catalogue record for this title is available from the British Library

ISBN: 978-1-4718-0225-6

3 2 1

2014 2013

Introduction

Study Skills – what you need to know to pass exams!

Pause for thought

Many students might skip quickly through a page like this. After all, we all know how to revise. Do you really though?

Think about this:

"IF YOU ALWAYS DO WHAT YOU ALWAYS DO, YOU WILL ALWAYS GET WHAT YOU HAVE ALWAYS GOT."

Do you like the grades you get? Do you want to do better? If you get full marks in your assessment, then that's great! Change nothing! This section is just to help you get that little bit better than you already are.

There are two main parts to the advice on offer here. The first part highlights fairly obvious things but which are also very important. The second part makes suggestions about revision that you might not have thought about but which WILL help you.

Part 1

DOH! It's so obvious but …

Start revising in good time

Don't leave it until the last minute – this will make you panic.

Make a revision timetable that sets out work time AND play time.

Sleep and eat!

Obvious really, and very helpful. Avoid arguments or stressful things too – even games that wind you up. You need to be fit, awake and focused!

Know your place!

Make sure you know exactly **WHEN and WHERE** your exams are.

Know your enemy!

Make sure you know what to expect in the exam.

How is the paper structured?

How much time is there for each question?

What types of question are involved?

Which topics seem to come up time and time again?

Which topics are your strongest and which are your weakest?

Are all topics compulsory or are there choices?

Learn by DOING!

There is no substitute for past papers and practice papers – they are simply essential! Tackling this collection of papers and answers is exactly the right thing to be doing as your exams approach.

Part 2

People learn in different ways. Some like low light, some bright. Some like early morning, some like evening / night. Some prefer warm, some prefer cold. But everyone uses their BRAIN and the brain works when it is active. Passive learning – sitting gazing at notes – is the most INEFFICIENT way to learn anything. Below you will find tips and ideas for making your revision more effective and maybe even more enjoyable. What follows gets your brain active, and active learning works!

Activity 1 – Stop and review

Step 1

When you have done no more than 5 minutes of revision reading STOP!

Step 2

Write a heading in your own words which sums up the topic you have been revising.

Step 3

Write a summary of what you have revised in no more than two sentences. Don't fool yourself by saying, 'I know it but I cannot put it into words'. That just means you don't know it well enough. If you cannot write your summary, revise that section again, knowing that you must write a summary at the end of it. Many of you will have notebooks full of blue/black ink writing. Many of the pages will not be especially attractive or memorable so try to liven them up a bit with colour as you are reviewing and rewriting. **This is a great memory aid, and memory is the most important thing.**

Activity 2 — Use technology!

Why should everything be written down? Have you thought about 'mental' maps, diagrams, cartoons and colour to help you learn? And rather than write down notes, why not record your revision material?

What about having a text message revision session with friends? Keep in touch with them to find out how and what they are revising and share ideas and questions.

Why not make a video diary where you tell the camera what you are doing, what you think you have learned and what you still have to do? No one has to see or hear it but the process of having to organise your thoughts in a formal way to explain something is a very important learning practice.

Be sure to make use of electronic files. You could begin to summarise your class notes. Your typing might be slow but it will get faster and the typed notes will be easier to read than the scribbles in your class notes. Try to add different fonts and colours to make your work stand out. You can easily Google relevant pictures, cartoons and diagrams which you can copy and paste to make your work more attractive and **MEMORABLE**.

Activity 3 – This is it. Do this and you will know lots!

Step 1

In this task you must be very honest with yourself! Find the SQA syllabus for your subject (www.sqa.org.uk). Look at how it is broken down into main topics called MANDATORY knowledge. That means stuff you MUST know.

Step 2

BEFORE you do ANY revision on this topic, write a list of everything that you already know about the subject. It might be quite a long list but you only need to write it once. It shows you all the information that is already in your long-term memory so you know what parts you do not need to revise!

Step 3

Pick a chapter or section from your book or revision notes. Choose a fairly large section or a whole chapter to get the most out of this activity.

With a buddy, use Skype, Facetime, Twitter or any other communication you have, to play the game "If this is the answer, what is the question?". For example, if you are revising Geography and the answer you provide is "meander", your buddy would have to make up a question like "What is the word that describes a feature of a river where it flows slowly and bends often from side to side?".

Make up 10 "answers" based on the content of the chapter or section you are using. Give this to your buddy to solve while you solve theirs.

Step 4

Construct a wordsearch of at least 10 X 10 squares. You can make it as big as you like but keep it realistic. Work together with a group of friends. Many apps allow you to make wordsearch puzzles online. The words and phrases can go in any direction and phrases can be split. Your puzzle must only contain facts linked to the topic you are revising. Your task is to find 10 bits of information to hide in your puzzle but you must not repeat information that you used in Step 3. DO NOT show where the words are. Fill up empty squares with random letters. Remember to keep a note of where your answers are hidden but do not show your friends. When you have a complete puzzle, exchange it with a friend to solve each other's puzzle.

Step 5

Now make up 10 questions (not "answers" this time) based on the same chapter used in the previous two tasks. Again, you must find NEW information that you have not yet used. Now it's getting hard to find that new information! Again, give your questions to a friend to answer.

Step 6

As you have been doing the puzzles, your brain has been actively searching for new information. Now write a NEW LIST that contains only the new information you have discovered when doing the puzzles. Your new list is the one to look at repeatedly for short bursts over the next few days. Try to remember more and more of it without looking at it. After a few days, you should be able to add words from your second list to your first list as you increase the information in your long-term memory.

FINALLY! Be inspired...

Make a list of different revision ideas and beside each one write **THINGS I HAVE** tried, **THINGS I WILL** try and **THINGS I MIGHT** try. Don't be scared of trying something new.

And remember – "FAIL TO PREPARE AND PREPARE TO FAIL!"

National 5 Modern Studies

The course

You will have studied the following three units:

- Democracy in Scotland and the United Kingdom
- Social Issues in the United Kingdom
- International Issues

Your teacher will usually have chosen one topic from each of the 3 sections above and you will answer questions on these in your exam (see table below).

SECTION 1	CHOICE ONE	CHOICE TWO
Democracy in Scotland and UK	A Democracy in Scotland	**OR** B Democracy in the UK
SECTION 2	CHOICE ONE	CHOICE TWO
Social Issues in the UK	C Social Inequality	**OR** D Crime and the Law
SECTION 3	CHOICE ONE	CHOICE TWO
International Issues	E World Powers	**OR** F World Issues

The Added Value unit for National 5 is an externally marked assessment. This consists of two parts:

- National 5 question paper
  60 marks allocated
  75% of marks

- National 5 assignment
  20 marks allocated
  25% of marks

Total marks available = 80

To gain the course award, all units and course assessments must be passed. The marks you achieve in the question paper and assignment are added together and an overall mark will indicate a pass or fail. From this, your course award will then be graded.

Question paper

You will have 1 hour and 30 minutes to complete the question paper, with a total of 60 marks allocated. There are 26 marks available for skills-based questions and 34 for knowledge and understanding, with 20 marks in total for each of the three exam sections as outlined in the table above.

In the exam paper, more marks are awarded for knowledge and understanding than skills so it is crucial that you have a sound grasp of content.

As stated, the paper will be divided into three sections, each worth 20 marks. Each section will have three questions. The three questions will be as follows:

Describe (worth either 4, 6 or 8 marks)
For example:
> Describe, in detail, at least two ways in which the police try to reduce crime levels.

Explain (worth either 4, 6 or 8 marks)
For example:
> Explain, in detail, why many people in the UK have good health while others do not.

Source-based (worth either out of 8 or 10)
For example:
> Using Sources 1, 2 and 3, what conclusions can be drawn about…?

What types of source-based questions will I need to answer?

There are three types of source-based skills questions and you will have practised these as class work. These three source-based skills questions are as follows:

- Using sources of information to identify and explain selective use of facts – this will have been assessed in your **Democracy in Scotland and UK unit**

- Using sources of information to make and justify a decision – this will have been assessed in your **Social Issues in the UK unit**

- Using sources of information to draw and support conclusions – this will have been assessed in your **International Issues unit.**

Remember, in your course exam the skills based questions can appear in any of the three units – so selective use of facts could be a question in the International Issues section of the exam.

Remember, in your course exam the knowledge and skills questions for International Issues will not refer to a particular country or issue. You will be expected to base your describe and explain answers around your knowledge and understanding of the World Power or World Issue you have studied.

What makes a good Knowledge and Understanding answer?

- Answer the question as set and only provide information relevant to the question.

- As far as you can, use up-to-date examples to illustrate your understanding of the question.

- Answer in detail and write in paragraphs with development of the points you wish to discuss. Remember, one very developed describe answer can gain 3 marks and one very developed explain answer can gain 4 marks.
- Show awareness of the difference between **describe** and **explain** questions and be able to answer appropriately.
- Use the number of marks given to each question as a guide to how much to write. Writing a long answer for a four mark question may cause you difficulty in completing the paper.

What makes a bad Knowledge and Understanding answer?

- Don't just write a list of facts. You will receive a maximum of two marks.
- Don't change the question to what you know – this is called *turning a question* and you will receive no marks for detailed description or explanation if it is not relevant.
- Avoid giving answers that are dated and too historical. This is especially a danger in the International Issues section.
- Don't rush together different issues, factors and explanations without developing your answer.

What makes a good Skills answer?

- Make full use of all the sources by linking evidence from more than one source to provide detailed arguments.
- Interpret statistical sources to indicate their significance to a question and how they link to other evidence.
- Make sure you use only the sources provided when writing your answers.

What makes a bad Skills answer?

- Don't use only a single piece of evidence from a source to provide argument.
- Don't simply repeat the statistical or written evidence without indicating its significance.
- Avoid bringing in your own knowledge of the issue or your own personal opinion.

Specific Skills advice

- For a selective use of facts answer, you should state whether the evidence being used is showing selectivity or not, and whether the evidence is supporting or opposing the view.
- For a conclusion answer, you should use the headings to draw an overall conclusion, which may be given at the beginning or end of the explanation.
- For a decision/recommendation answer, you should justify your decision and explain why you have rejected the other option.

So you are now ready to answer the exam questions.

Good luck!

Remember that the rewards for passing National 5 Modern Studies are well worth it! Your pass will help you get the future you want for yourself. In the exam, be confident in your own ability. If you're not sure how to answer a question, trust your instincts and just give it a go anyway. Keep calm and don't panic! GOOD LUCK!

2013 Specimen Question Paper

N5

National
Qualifications
SPECIMEN ONLY

Mark

SQ31/N5/01

Modern Studies

Date — Not applicable

Duration — 1 hour and 30 minutes

Fill in these boxes and read what is printed below.

Full name of centre

Town

Forename(s)

Surname

Number of seat

Date of birth

Day	Month	Year
D D	M M	Y Y

Scottish candidate number

Total marks — 60

SECTION 1 — DEMOCRACY IN SCOTLAND AND THE UNITED KINGDOM — 20 marks

Attempt ONE part, EITHER

Part A Democracy in Scotland   Pages 2–4
OR
Part B Democracy in the United Kingdom   Pages 5–7

SECTION 2 — SOCIAL ISSUES IN THE UNITED KINGDOM — 20 marks

Attempt ONE part, EITHER

Part C Social Inequality   Pages 8–10
OR
Part D Crime and the Law   Pages 11–13

SECTION 3 — INTERNATIONAL ISSUES — 20 marks

Attempt ONE part, EITHER

Part E World Powers   Pages 14–16
OR
Part F World Issues   Pages 17–19

Before attempting the questions you must check that your answer booklet is for the same subject and level as this question paper.

Read the questions carefully.

On the answer booklet, you must clearly identify the question number you are attempting.

Use **blue** or **black** ink.

Before leaving the examination room you must give your answer booklet to the Invigilator.
If you do not, you may lose all the marks for this paper.

SECTION 1 — DEMOCRACY IN SCOTLAND AND THE UNITED KINGDOM — 20 marks

Attempt ONE part, either

Part A — Democracy in Scotland   on pages 2–4

OR

Part B — Democracy in the United Kingdom   on pages 5–7

PART A — DEMOCRACY IN SCOTLAND

In your answers to Questions 1 and 2 you should give recent examples from Scotland.

Question 1

Groups which try to influence the Scottish Government		
Pressure Groups	Trade Unions	The Media

Choose **one** of the groups above.

Describe, **in detail**, **two** ways in which the group you have chosen tries to influence the Scottish Government.

4

Question 2

> The Additional Member System (AMS), used to elect the Scottish Parliament, has both advantages and disadvantages.

Explain, **in detail**, the advantages **and** disadvantages of the Additional Member System (AMS) which is used to elect the Scottish Parliament.

8

MARKS | DO NOT WRITE IN THIS MARGIN

Part A (continued)

Question 3

Study Sources 1, 2 and 3 below, then attempt the question which follows.

SOURCE 1

Committees in the Scottish Parliament

Much of the important work of the Scottish Parliament goes on in the many committees set up by the Parliament. In session 2008–09 the committees completed inquiries into a range of subjects, including tourism, child poverty, fuel poverty, and flooding and flood management in Scotland. In addition, the committees' job is to closely check the work of the Scottish Government and any of its proposed laws. Committee meetings have taken place in venues around Scotland, including Fraserburgh, Ayr and Aberdeen.

Committees can request debating time in the Scottish Parliament to bring issues raised in reports they have published to the attention of a wider audience. The Public Petitions Committee, for example, debated its report on the availability, on the National Health Service (NHS), of cancer treatment drugs. Committees also have the right to put forward Bills, hoping they will become law. One Bill out of the 17 introduced in 2008–09 —on a pension scheme for MSPs—was a Committee Bill.

The membership of the committees is made up of MSPs from every party, with Committee Conveners, who chair meetings, being drawn from different parties. Most committees meet weekly or fortnightly, usually on Tuesdays or on Wednesday mornings, in one of the Scottish Parliament's committee rooms—or in locations around Scotland. Most meetings are open to the public.

Committees play a central part in the work of the Parliament—taking evidence from witnesses, examining proposed new laws and conducting inquiries. The work of the committees has contributed to the positive view most Scots have of their Parliament, with 70% saying devolution had been good for Scotland after 10 years.

SOURCE 2

Scottish Parliament Committees by Convener's Party 2008–09

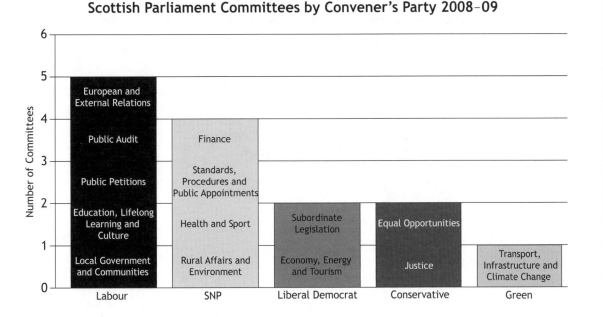

Part A Question 3 (continued)

SOURCE 3

Case Study: Public Petitions Committee

- The public petitions system gives members of the public direct access to policy development and the chance to examine new laws.

- The Public Petitions Committee has nine members: three Labour, three SNP, and one each from the Conservatives, Liberal Democrats and the Green Party.

- The existence of the Public Petitions Committee means the public can raise issues of concern directly with their Parliament.

- During 2008–09, 112 new petitions were lodged; the committee heard oral evidence on 35 new petitions and considered over 200 current petitions.

- The committee launched a year-long inquiry investigating ways to increase public awareness of, and participation in, the petitions process.

- It took forward an inquiry into the availability of cancer treatment drugs on the NHS.

- It hosted a debate in the chamber of the Parliament where community groups, victims, police, medical staff and many others met to discuss knife crime.

- The Public Petitions Committee played an important part in the successful law banning smoking in public places.

- The e-petitions system, which allows petitions to be raised online, continued to be influential, with around two-thirds of petitions being lodged in this way.

- Members of the public have lodged over 1,244 petitions in the past ten years.

Using Sources 1, 2 and 3 above, what **conclusions** can be drawn about committees in the Scottish Parliament?

You should reach a conclusion about each of the following:

- the work done by committees

- the membership of committees

- public involvement in committees.

Your conclusions must be supported by evidence from the sources. You should link information within and between sources in support of your conclusions.

Your answer must be based on all three sources.

8

NOW GO TO SECTION 2 ON *PAGE EIGHT*

MARKS | DO NOT WRITE IN THIS MARGIN

PART B — DEMOCRACY IN THE UNITED KINGDOM

In your answers to Questions 1 and 2 you should give recent examples from the United Kingdom.

Question 1

Groups which try to influence the United Kingdom Government		
Pressure Groups	Trade Unions	The Media

Choose **one** of the groups above.

Describe, **in detail**, **two** ways in which the group you have chosen tries to influence the UK Government.

4

Question 2

> The First Past the Post system (FPTP), used to elect the United Kingdom Parliament, has both advantages and disadvantages.

Explain, **in detail**, the advantages **and** disadvantages of the First Past the Post system (FPTP) which is used to elect the United Kingdom Parliament.

8

MARKS | DO NOT WRITE IN THIS MARGIN

Part B (continued)

Question 3

Study Sources 1, 2 and 3 below, then attempt the question which follows.

SOURCE 1

Committees in the UK Parliament

Some of the most important work of the House of Commons goes on in the many Select Committees. Select Committees examine the work of Government. They keep a close eye on the expenditure, administration and policy of every Government department. Over the years, this checking role of the Select Committees has become well-established and well-publicised.

Committees are normally made up of backbench MPs. Their membership reflects the strength of each party in the House of Commons. This means the governing party always has a majority. Select Committees can hold meetings in different parts of the country, members of the public can attend, each has its own website and committee meetings are broadcast on television and the Internet.

Committees play a central part in the work of Parliament—taking evidence from witnesses including senior Government members, examining proposed new laws and conducting inquiries. MPs from every party take part in the work of the committees with Committee Chairpersons being drawn from different parties. In 2010, for the first time, Committee Chairs were elected by their fellow MPs.

Most committee reports are unanimous (ie publicly supported by all committee members), reflecting a more non-party way of working. Different parties often work together and try to reach agreement in the committees. While the reputation of Parliament as a whole has suffered in recent years, the work of the Select Committees is seen as a real check on the power of Government.

SOURCE 2

UK Parliament Select Committees by Chairperson's party 2008–09

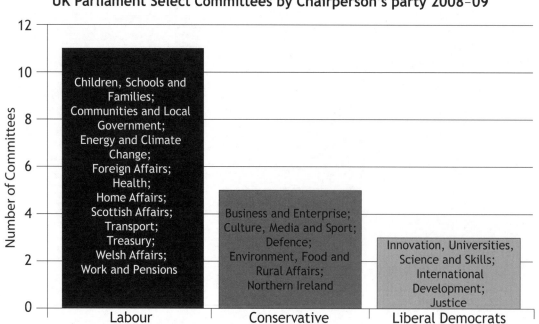

MARKS | DO NOT WRITE IN THIS MARGIN

Part B Question 3 (continued)

SOURCE 3

Case Study: Treasury Select Committee

- The Treasury Select Committee took a leading role in investigating the financial and banking crisis of 2008–09.

- In 2009, the Treasury Select Committee had 14 members: eight Labour, four Conservatives and two Liberal Democrats.

- The Committee chooses its own subjects of inquiry. An inquiry may last for several months and result in a report to the House of Commons; or consist of a single day's evidence which may be published without a report.

- When the Committee has chosen an inquiry it normally contacts the media outlining the main themes of inquiry and inviting interested individuals, groups and organisations to submit written evidence.

- Parliament has given the Committee the power to send for "persons, papers and records". It therefore has powers to insist upon the attendance of witnesses, such as Ministers and civil servants, and the production of papers and other material.

- Members of the public are welcome to attend hearings of the Committee.

- July 2009, the Treasury Select Committee announced a new inquiry: "Women in the City" and called for evidence.

- At a televised hearing of the Treasury Select Committee, former Royal Bank of Scotland chief executive, Sir Fred Goodwin, told MPs he "could not be more sorry" for what had happened during the banking crisis.

- The Treasury Select Committee was successful in putting pressure, along with others, on the Government to help those affected by the ending of the 10p rate of income tax.

Using Sources 1, 2 and 3 above, what **conclusions** can be drawn about committees in the UK Parliament?

You should reach a conclusion about each of the following:

- the work done by committees

- the membership of committees

- public involvement in committees.

Your conclusions must be supported by evidence from the sources. You should link information within and between sources in support of your conclusions.   8

NOW GO TO SECTION 2 ON *PAGE EIGHT*

MARKS | DO NOT WRITE IN THIS MARGIN

SECTION 2 — SOCIAL ISSUES IN THE UNITED KINGDOM — 20 marks

Attempt ONE part, either

Part C — Social Inequality   on pages 8–10

OR

Part D — Crime and the Law   on pages 11–13

PART C — SOCIAL INEQUALITY

In your answers to Questions 1 and 2 you should give recent examples from the United Kingdom.

Question 1

Examples of some groups that face inequality		
Ethnic minority groups	Elderly people	Unemployed people
Lone parent families	Disabled groups	Women

Choose **one** group from above or another group you have studied.

Describe, **in detail**, at least two ways in which the Government provides help for the group you have chosen.

6

Question 2

Many people in the UK have good health while others do not.

Explain, **in detail**, why many people in the UK have good health while others do not.

6

MARKS | DO NOT WRITE IN THIS MARGIN

Part C (continued)

Question 3

Study Sources 1, 2 and 3 below, then attempt the question which follows.

SOURCE 1

Homelessness in Scotland

- In Scotland, it is the responsibility of local councils to help homeless people.
- In 2011–12, 45,322 households made homeless applications to their local council in Scotland. In 2010–11 the figure was 56,350.
- In 2011–12, local councils accepted 35,515 of these applications. In 2010–11 the figure was 38,100.
- Police report that the number of people forced onto homeless waiting lists because of their anti-social neighbours has doubled since 2001.
- At present there are 87,000 empty homes of all types across Scotland and 29,300 second and holiday homes which lie empty for much of the year.
- Many believe that the homelessness problem worsened due to the introduction of the "Right to Buy" policy. This allowed council tenants to buy their homes, leaving few decent houses for rental.
- Housing charity Shelter has recently criticised the Scottish Government for cutting the housing budget by 45%. Shelter claims that the most needy and vulnerable groups are suffering.
- In 2012, council waiting lists had almost 188,000 households on them. At the same time there were 7,847 empty council houses.
- In 2011–12, 15,900 new houses were completed in Scotland. This represents a reduction of 38% over the last four years.
- Charities like APEX and SACRO try to help ex-prisoners who find themselves homeless. Both organisations have limited funding.

SOURCE 2

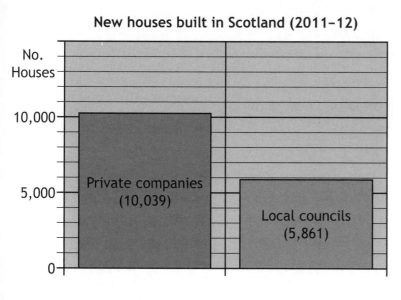

New houses built in Scotland (2011–12)

No. Houses — Private companies (10,039); Local councils (5,861). Scale marked at 0, 5,000, 10,000.

Local council homes sold through "Right to Buy" since 2001	
City	Houses sold through "Right to Buy"
Aberdeen	4,345
Dundee	2,017
Edinburgh	3,914
Glasgow	8,566
Rest of Scotland	61,569
Scottish Total	80,411

Part C Question 3 (continued)

SOURCE 3

Article by Daisy Kingscourt, homeless campaigner

Although homelessness is falling in Scotland, it is still a worrying problem. Being without a permanent home causes stress and illness among people. It affects the large number of children involved, damaging their education and their health.

Over one quarter of all the households who apply for homeless status do so as a result of a family dispute. The fact that 5% of homeless people have left prison or some kind of hospital only to find themselves on the streets is a scandal. Homeless Scots do not often match the common view of the homeless, ie a person who has been evicted for not paying their rent or mortgage. In fact, less than 5% of the Scottish homeless are without a home for this reason. Worryingly, 5% of homeless people leave their homes as a result of violence or harassment from their neighbours. Working together, the Government, police and local councils must solve these problems. An easy first step would be to reverse recent Scottish Government spending cuts which are clearly affecting these vulnerable groups.

Using Sources 1, 2 and 3 above explain why the view of Danny Wilson is **selective in the use of facts**.

"**The homeless problem in Scotland is caused by a lack of available houses.**"

View of Danny Wilson.

- You should give information that Danny Wilson has selected as it supports his view.

- You should give information that Danny Wilson has not selected as it does not support his view.

Your answer must be based on all three sources.

8

NOW GO TO SECTION 3 ON *PAGE FOURTEEN*

MARKS | DO NOT WRITE IN THIS MARGIN

PART D — CRIME AND THE LAW

In your answers to Questions 1 and 2 you should give recent examples from the United Kingdom.

Question 1

The police in the UK try to reduce crime levels.

Describe, **in detail**, at least two ways in which the police try to reduce crime levels.

6

Question 2

There are many reasons why people commit crime.

Explain, **in detail**, why some people commit crime.

6

Part D (continued)

Question 3

Study Sources 1, 2 and 3 below, then attempt the question which follows.

SOURCE 1

Facts and Viewpoints

The Scottish Government is considering a petition which would mean that any person carrying a knife would be given a mandatory custodial sentence. This would mean that possession of such a weapon would automatically result in the offender being sent to prison or detention centre.

- Community groups have called on the Government to take action to deter young people from carrying knives.
- 1,200 offenders were sentenced for possession of a knife between 2004 and 2009, but only 314 were given custodial sentences.
- Scottish Prisons reported that as a result of overcrowding, offenders were not serving their full sentence and were being released early. Automatic sentences may make this problem worse.
- In 2009, one in five people convicted of carrying a knife in Edinburgh had previously been charged for a similar offence.
- Thirty per cent of young people thought that introducing tougher sentences would reduce knife crime; 53% thought that community sentences were an appropriate punishment for young people found carrying a knife.
- Judges in Scotland think that they should be able to consider the personal circumstances of each case before sentencing.
- A custodial sentence can have a huge impact on the future of young people convicted.
- The number of people sent to prison for carrying a knife fell to a five-year low in 2008 because only one in three offenders were jailed.
- In 2009, 78% of youths questioned in Glasgow said that a prison sentence would make them never carry a knife again.

SOURCE 2

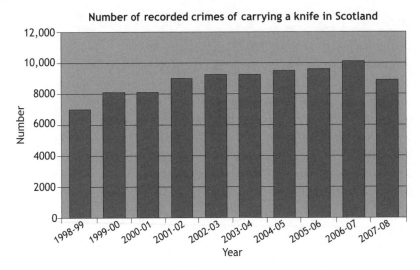

Number of recorded crimes of carrying a knife in Scotland

MARKS

Part D Question 3 (continued)

SOURCE 3

Evidence of Louise McKay to Scottish Parliament Committee

Locking up people who carry knives is not the answer to tackling this problem. Many of the young people who carry knives are not criminals. Sending these youngsters to prison would simply punish them for the rest of their lives for being young and foolish. Keeping a prisoner locked up costs around £30,000 per year. Even half of this money spent on community projects would help young people realise how much damage they can do themselves and others by carrying a knife. The numbers caught carrying knives in Scotland is falling. Clearly, this Government's proposal for an automatic prison sentence is not necessary and would be a waste of taxpayers' money.

Using Sources 1, 2 and 3 above explain why the view of Billy Mackenzie is **selective in the use of facts.**

> Giving anyone caught carrying a knife a prison sentence is a good way to reduce knife crime.
>
> **View of Billy Mackenzie.**

- You should give information that Billy Mackenzie has selected as it supports his view.
- You should give information that Billy Mackenzie has not selected as it does not support his view.

Your answer must be based on all three sources.   8

NOW GO TO SECTION 3 ON *PAGE FOURTEEN*

SECTION 3 — INTERNATIONAL ISSUES — 20 marks

Attempt ONE part, either

Part E—World Powers　　　on pages 14–16

OR

Part F—World Issues　　　on pages 17–19

PART E — WORLD POWERS

In your answers to Questions 1 and 2 you should give recent examples from a world power you have studied.

Question 1

> Citizens can participate in politics in many ways.

Describe, **in detail**, **two** ways in which citizens from a world power you have studied can participate in politics.

4

Question 2

> Social and economic inequalities exist in all world powers.

Explain, **in detail**, why social and economic inequalities exist in a world power you have studied.

6

MARKS | DO NOT WRITE IN THIS MARGIN

Part E (continued)

Question 3

Study Sources 1, 2 and 3 below, then attempt the question which follows.

You are a government adviser. You have been asked to recommend whether the Government should build the Melo Bonte Dam.

Option 1	Option 2
Build the Melo Bonte Dam	Do not build the Melo Bonte Dam

SOURCE 1

Government Signs Contracts for Controversial Rainforest Dam

In July 2010, a South American Government signed contracts for the construction of a massive new hydroelectric dam in their rainforest. Once complete, Melo Bonte will be the world's third-largest hydroelectric dam. The Minister of Mines and Energy said the Melo Bonte complex, to be built near the mouth of the Celdy River in the northern rainforest, will "play an important role in the development of the area and people displaced by the dam will be compensated".

The project has raised a storm of protest, with many judges, Hollywood celebrities, environmental pressure groups and organisations representing rainforest residents, opposing it. In April 2010, *Avatar* director James Cameron and two members of the film's cast took part in protests about the dam. Protesters say the proposed dam would cause "serious damage" to the rainforest ecosystem and the lives of up to 50,000 rainforest residents could be affected as 500 square kilometres could be flooded.

The Government says the dam is vital for the continued expansion of the economy, as the growing population needs more electricity. The Melo Bonte Dam is expected to provide electricity for 23 million homes. The companies awarded contracts to build the dam will have to pay large amounts to protect the environment. The Government said that most people support the decision to build the dam.

The dam has been defended by some of the rainforest's residents who hope to benefit from the estimated 18,000 direct jobs and 80,000 indirect jobs the project will create. However, some experts and business representatives in the energy industry also oppose the dam. They say the actual cost will be 60% higher than its US$10·8 billion budget and will only operate at 40% of its capacity due to the drop in water in the Celdy River during the dry season.

Part E Question 3 (continued)

SOURCE 2

Results of Opinion Polls

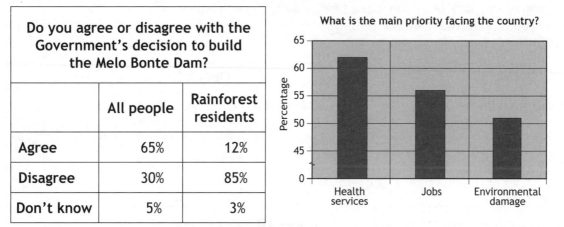

Do you agree or disagree with the Government's decision to build the Melo Bonte Dam?		
	All people	**Rainforest residents**
Agree	65%	12%
Disagree	30%	85%
Don't know	5%	3%

What is the main priority facing the country?

(Bar chart — Percentage (y-axis 0, 45, 50, 55, 60, 65): Health services ~62, Jobs ~56, Environmental damage ~51)

SOURCE 3

Melo Bonte Dam Protests: April–July

April 12	International celebrities attend protests along with over 500 protesters to demand the cancellation of the project to build the Melo Bonte dam.
April 15	Under pressure from local people and campaigners, local politicians in the area obtain a court injunction to ban companies from bidding to build the dam.
April 17	The Government wins an appeal to overturn the ban in a higher court.
April 18	500 Greenpeace protesters dump three tons of manure in front of the National Electric Energy Agency in the capital city.
May 19	The Government finally wins the court case and awards the US$10 billion contract to a group of nine companies who hope to be transmitting power.
June 17	Kayapo Indians, who live in the rainforest, blockade a major highway disrupting commercial goods traffic.
June 20	Many people who live in the rainforest back the dam because it will generate employment to replace the jobs lost since a clampdown on illegal logging.
July 2	Campaigners say they will continue protesting despite the contract being awarded.
July 15	The companies building the dam agree to pay US$803 million to create parks and help monitor forests and to pay compensation to people affected by the dam.

You must decide which option to recommend, **either** build the Melo Bonte Dam **(Option 1) or** do not build the Melo Bonte Dam **(Option 2)**.

   (i) Using Sources 1, 2 and 3 above and opposite, **which option would you choose?**

   (ii) Give reasons to **support** your choice.

   (iii) **Explain** why you did not choose the other option.

Your answer must be based on all three sources.

10

MARKS | DO NOT WRITE IN THIS MARGIN

PART F — WORLD ISSUES

In your answers to Questions 1 and 2 you should give recent examples from a world issue you have studied.

Question 1

International organisations which try to resolve international issues and problems		
United Nations Organisation	NATO	World Bank
European Union	African Union	Charities and other NGOs

Describe, **in detail**, **two** ways in which international organisations try to resolve an international issue or problem you have studied.   **4**

Question 2

International issues and problems have many causes.

Explain, **in detail**, the causes of an international issue or problem you have studied.   **6**

Part F (continued)

Question 3

Study Sources 1, 2 and 3 below, then attempt the question which follows.

You are an adviser to the European Union (EU). You have been asked to recommend whether Country A or Country B should be allowed to join the EU.

Option 1	**Option 2**
Allow Country "A" to join the EU	Allow Country "B" to join the EU

Country A and Country B are **Candidate Countries** hoping to be allowed to join the European Union. Source 1 and 2 contain information about both countries taken from their applications.

SOURCE 1

CANDIDATE COUNTRY "A"

- This country has a small population of 4·5 million people and an average income of only €11,200.

- The police have worked hard to catch drug traffickers. Many have been given long jail sentences.

- Country A allows its citizens many rights and freedoms. It would meet the criteria of the European Convention on Human Rights.

- UNICEF and several large childrens' charities have criticised Country A for its social care system. Investigations have shown that many elderly people and children are cared for in terrible conditions.

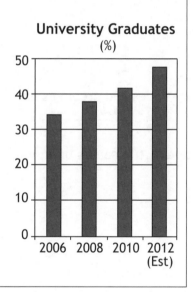

University Graduates (%)

SOURCE 2

CANDIDATE COUNTRY "B"

- Country B produces 32 million barrels of oil per day and only uses 13 million barrels. It wants to export more.

- Healthcare is poor in Country B. Life expectancy is low at 58 and child mortality is high at 11 per 1,000 live births.

- In Country B, 36% of the population still work on farms. The EU would be asked to spend money to improve agriculture.

- UNESCO has praised the primary education system in Country B as levels of illiteracy have fallen to below 10%.

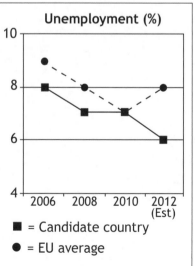

Unemployment (%)

■ = Candidate country
● = EU average

MARKS

Part F Question 3 (continued)

SOURCE 3

EUROPEAN UNION (EU) FACTFILE

- The EU has grown over the years. In 2009, it had 27 member states and a population close to 500 million. Average life expectancy in the EU is 78 years and child mortality is 5 per 1,000 live births. More countries still wish to join.

- 48% of the EU's budget is spent supporting agriculture and fishing although these industries employ only 4% of the workforce. This support is planned to fall over the next few years and many member governments see this as a necessity.

- The EU's growing economy needs more university graduates. EU countries are among the most technologically advanced in the world. At the moment, 51% of school leavers go to university.

- Across all member states, schools in the EU have achieved a 96% literacy level. Any country wishing to join must be able to come close to this figure.

- Trade between EU member states contributes to the high standard of living within the EU. On average, a worker in the EU earns €23,100. Several member states are concerned about the number of poor countries applying to join.

- The EU has to import 11 million barrels of oil every day from countries like Russia. Many people in the EU worry that it is too dependent on Russia for oil and would like to admit new members with large oil reserves.

- EU health and welfare systems are among the best in the world. Groups such as the elderly and children are well looked after. Any new members must try to match these standards.

Survey of EU Public Opinion

Question: How important is it that new EU members have:

	Unimportant	Not very important	Fairly important	Very important
Strict policies on crime?	4%	8%	38%	50%
Low unemployment?	0%	0%	48%	52%
A good record on human rights?	2%	10%	53%	35%

You must decide which option to recommend, **either** allow Country A to join the EU **(Option 1)** or allow Country B to join the EU **(Option 2).**

   (i)   Using Sources 1, 2 and 3 above, **which option would you choose**?

   (ii)   Give reasons to **support** your choice.

   (iii)   **Explain** why you did not choose the other option.

Your answer must be based on all three sources.

10

National Qualifications
MODEL PAPER 1

Modern Studies

Duration — 1 hour and 30 minutes

Total marks — 60

SECTION 1 — DEMOCRACY IN SCOTLAND AND THE UNITED KINGDOM — 20 marks

Attempt ONE part, EITHER

SECTION 2 — SOCIAL ISSUES IN THE UNITED KINGDOM — 20 marks

Attempt ONE part, EITHER

SECTION 3 — INTERNATIONAL ISSUES — 20 marks

Attempt ONE part, EITHER

Before attempting the questions you must check that your answer booklet is for the same subject and level as this question paper.

Read the questions carefully.

On the answer booklet, you must clearly identify the question number you are attempting.

Use **blue** or **black** ink.

Before leaving the examination room you must give your answer booklet to the Invigilator.
If you do not, you may lose all the marks for this paper.

MARKS | DO NOT WRITE IN THIS MARGIN

SECTION 1 — DEMOCRACY IN SCOTLAND AND THE UNITED KINGDOM — 20 marks

Attempt ONE part, either

Part A — Democracy in Scotland   on pages 2–4

OR

Part B — Democracy in the United Kingdom   on pages 5–7

Part A — Democracy in Scotland

In your answers to Questions 1 and 2 you should give recent examples from Scotland.

Question 1

> Decisions made about local services by councils can affect the lives of people in Scotland.

Describe, **in detail, two** ways in which decisions made about local services by councils can affect the lives of people in Scotland.   **4**

Question 2

> The Additional Member System (AMS) is used to elect the Scottish Parliament. Some people are happy with the way AMS has worked while others are unhappy.

Explain, **in detail**, why some people are happy with the way the Additional Member System (AMS) of voting has worked while others are unhappy.   **8**

NOW ATTEMPT QUESTION 3

Part A (continued)

MARKS

Question 3

Study Sources 1, 2 and 3 below, then attempt the question which follows.

SOURCE 1

New Tax Powers Proposed for Scottish Parliament

More than 10 years after devolution was introduced in Scotland, there have been calls for more powers to be given to the Scottish Parliament. Greater tax raising powers have been proposed for the Parliament. The new proposal would work by cutting the amount of money, from the block grant, which the Scottish Government receives from the UK Government and reducing the rate of income tax in Scotland by 10p. MSPs would then have to decide what to do:

- either set the "Scottish tax rate" at 10p so the amount of cash Scotland will get would stay the same

- or cut the rate to less than 10p and people's taxes would fall but there would be a reduction in public spending

- or set a tax rate higher than 10p and be able to spend more on public services.

Some have argued against this change as it could lead to higher taxes in Scotland compared to England. It may also as stated give the UK government an excuse to reduce the funding to the Scottish Government and Parliament. This financial reduction could lead to a crisis in our hospitals and schools given the significant cuts already made to the public sector. It could lead to a decrease in the Scottish public's trust of the Scottish Government

Supporters of the proposal see it as the next step to increase the powers of the devolved Parliament now that it is well established and trusted by the Scottish people. It would also make the Parliament more accountable, as voters would be able to choose the party which had the tax and spending policies they support. There would be fewer arguments between the UK Government and the Scottish Government about money as the Scottish Government would now have greater control over its own spending decisions.

SOURCE 2

Public Opinion Survey: Who has the most influence over the way Scotland is run?

	1999	2001	2003	2005	2007	2009
Scottish Government/ Scottish Parliament	13%	15%	17%	23%	28%	33%
United Kingdom Government/United Kingdom Parliament	66%	66%	64%	47%	47%	39%

Part A Question 3 (continued)

SOURCE 3

Percentage of people who trust the UK and Scottish Governments to act in Scotland's interests

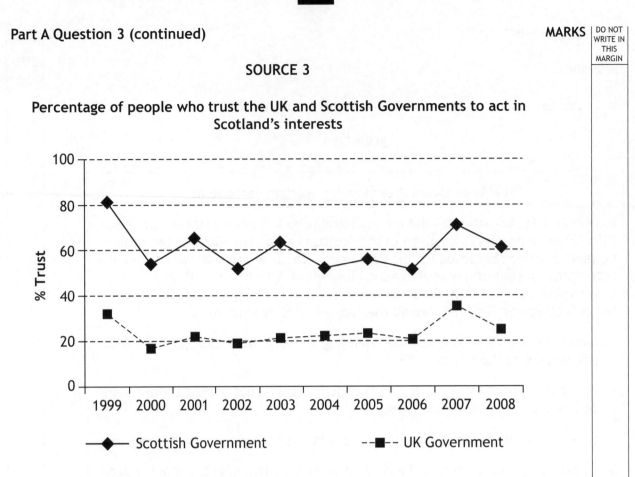

— ◆ — Scottish Government   – – ■ – – UK Government

Using Sources 1, 2 and 3 above, explain why the view of Gillian Duffy is **selective in the use of facts.**

> **New tax raising powers for the Scottish Parliament would be good for Scotland.**
>
> **View of Gillian Duffy**

In your answer you must:

give evidence from the sources that support Gillian Duffy's view

and

give evidence from the sources that opposes Gillian Duffy's view

Your answer must be based on all three sources.   8

NOW GO TO SECTION 2 ON *PAGE EIGHT*

PART B — DEMOCRACY IN THE UNITED KINGDOM

In your answers to Questions 1 and 2 you should give recent examples from the United Kingdom.

Question 1

> The House of Lords plays a part in decision making in the UK.

Describe, **in detail**, **two** ways in which the House of Lords plays a part in decision making in the UK.

4

Question 2

Media	Trade Unions	Pressure Groups

Choose **one** of the above.

Explain, **in detail**, why some people think they play a positive role in politics while others believe they play a negative role in politics.

8

Part B (continued)

Question 3

Study Sources 1, 2 and 3 below, then attempt the question which follows.

SOURCE 1

Party Leaders' Debates Change Election Campaign

When the General Election was called for in April 2010, many people thought that the campaign would be of little interest. The Conservative Party had been far ahead of Labour in the opinion polls for many months. It was predicted that David Cameron and the Conservative Party would win the election. For the first time in the UK, televised leaders' debates were held. The three main political parties agreed to hold three debates involving Gordon Brown (Labour), David Cameron (Conservative) and Nick Clegg (Liberal Democrats). The first debate had a major impact on the opinion polls; Nick Clegg was thought to have done well. His strong performance, compared to the other leaders, saw the Liberal Democrats rise in the opinion polls and turned a "two horse race" between Labour and the Conservatives into a real contest between the three parties.

Many people felt the debates focused too much on the personality of the leaders at the expense of local campaigns; and image and style were seen to be more important than policies. Some people believed the debates would have little impact on the result as most people had made up their minds, before the election, about who they would vote for Millions of viewers watched the debates and turnout increased in the 2010 election to 65·1%, up 4% on 2005. Labour lost the election; Gordon Brown was thought to have done poorly in the debates. After the votes were counted, no party had an overall majority so a coalition government was formed by the Conservative Party, which was the largest party, and the Liberal Democrats. David Cameron became Prime Minister with Nick Clegg as his deputy.

SOURCE 2

Do you think the leaders' debates were a positive or negative change to the election campaign?

Did the leaders' debates make a difference to how you cast your vote at the general election?

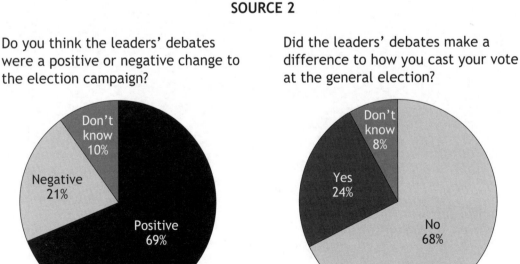

Part B Question 3 (continued)   MARKS

DO NOT WRITE IN THIS MARGIN

SOURCE 3

Who do you think performed best overall in the party leaders' debates?			
	1st debate	2nd debate	3rd debate
Gordon Brown (Labour)	19%	29%	25%
David Cameron (Conservative)	29%	36%	41%
Nick Clegg (Liberal Democrats)	51%	32%	32%
Number of viewers (Channel debate shown on)	9·4m (ITV)	4·1m (Sky)	8·4m (BBC)

All figures from YouGov

Using Sources 1, 2 and 3 above, explain why the view of Adam Stewart is **selective in the use of facts.**

> **The party leaders' debates in the 2010 election had little impact on the election campaign.**
>
> **View of Adam Stewart**

In your answer you must:

give evidence from the sources that support Adam Stewart's view

and

give evidence from the sources that opposes Adam Stewart's view

Your answer must be based on all three sources.   8

NOW GO TO SECTION 2 ON *PAGE EIGHT*

MARKS

SECTION 2 — SOCIAL ISSUES THE UNITED KINGDOM — 20 marks

Attempt ONE part, either

Part C — Social Inequality　　　　　　　on pages 8–11

OR

Part D — Crime and the Law　　　　　　on pages 12–14

PART C — SOCIAL INEQUALITY

In your answers to Questions 1 and 2 you should give recent examples from Scotland.

Question 1

Government has tried to improve the health of people in Scotland.

Describe, **in detail**, **two** ways in which the Government has tried to improve the health of people in Scotland.　　　　**4**

Question 2

Some people live in poverty in the United Kingdom.

Explain, **in detail**, why some people live in poverty in the United Kingdom.　　　　**6**

Part C (continued)

Question 3

Study Sources 1, 2 and 3 below, then attempt the question which follows.

You are an adviser to the UK Government. You have been asked to recommend whether or not the Government should continue with the system of Working Tax Credits (WTC) as part of Universal Credit or not to continue with the system.

Option 1 Continue with the system of Working Tax Credits.	**Option 2** Do not continue with the system of Working Tax Credits.

SOURCE 1

Facts and Viewpoints

Working Tax Credit (WTC), introduced in 2003, can be given to top up earnings if a person is in work but on low pay. You can get WTC if you are over 16 years old and work more than 16 hours per week and are also either a parent or responsible for children.

- Working Tax Credits help people to beat the poverty trap—it makes sure a person's income is better in work than out of work and living on benefits.

- There have been problems in the system with overpayments being made and then having to be paid back.

- The basic amount awarded is £1,730 per year with extra payments depending on circumstances.

- Many families have suffered hardship when attempts have been made to recover overpayments made to them, which many poor families have already spent.

- In 2005, the Working Tax Credit website was closed down because of a high level of fraudulent claims by organised criminals.

- Working Tax Credits have been criticised as they encourage employers to pay low wages.

- Over half a million children have been lifted out of poverty as more people on low or moderate incomes have been helped; more than through any other single measure.

- Over half the overpayment errors made affected those in the lowest income group—the very people who will struggle to pay them back.

- Working Tax Credit allows families to get back up to 80% of the cost of child care allowing adults to go back to work; this can be as much as £175 per week for one child and up to £300 per week for two or more children.

Part C Question 3 (continued)

SOURCE 2

Error and Fraud in Working Tax Credit System (2004–2005)

	Number of Cases of Error and Fraud	Amount Involved in Error and Fraud
2005	1,460,000	£2,440 million
2010	1,400,000	£2,660 million

Number of Children in Poverty: 2001–2010

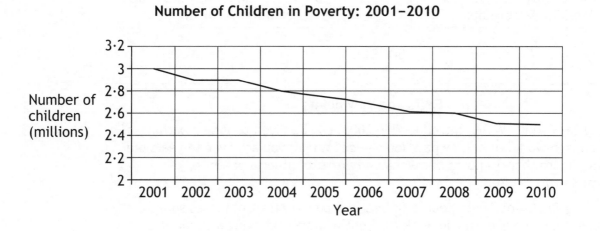

Part C Question 3 (continued)

SOURCE 3

Viewpoints

The Government should not continue with the system of Working Tax Credits. To date, the personal details of over 10,000 public sector workers had been stolen by organised tax criminals to be used to claim tax credits. Fraud and mistakes led to huge losses. People have to notify the tax authorities when their pay rises. If they do not do this then they have to pay the overpaid WTC back. The stress that this has caused families can have a damaging effect on the children. Working Tax Credit should be scrapped and replaced by a simpler system.

Pressure Group Spokesperson

The Government should continue with the system of Working Tax Credits. In the past when people went from benefits to work they lost some means-tested benefits. The problem faced by many was that if they came off benefits and went into low paid jobs, they were worse off. There was little to motivate people to find work. Working Tax Credits encourage people to work and also give help with child care costs. Despite problems with overpayments in the first few years, many of these difficulties have now been sorted. The tax credit system has helped many families to get out of poverty.

Government Spokesperson

You must decide which option to recommend to the Government, **either** to continue with the system of Working Tax Credits **(Option 1) or** not to continue with the system of Working Tax Credits **(Option 2)**.

(i) Using Sources 1, 2 and 3 above and opposite, **which option would you choose?**

(ii) Give reasons to **support** your choice.

(iii) **Explain** why you did not choose the other option.

Your answer must be based on all three sources.

10

NOW GO TO SECTION 3 ON *PAGE FIFTEEN*

PART D — CRIME AND THE LAW

In your answers to Questions 1 and 2 you should give recent examples from the United Kingdom.

Question 1

> Some young people commit crimes.

Describe, **in detail**, **two** crimes most commonly committed by young people.

4

Question 2

> In some areas community policing is the best way to tackle crime, while in others the use of CCTV cameras is better.

Explain, **in detail**, why in some areas community policing is the best way to tackle crime, while in others the use of CCTV cameras is better.

6

Part D (continued)

Question 3

Study Sources 1, 2 and 3 below, then attempt the question which follows.

You are an adviser to the Scottish Government. You have been asked to recommend whether the DNA database should contain profiles of the whole population or keep the DNA database for profiles of convicted criminals only.

Option 1 The DNA database should contain profiles of the whole population.	**Option 2** The DNA database should contain profiles of convicted criminals only.

SOURCE 1

Facts and Viewpoints

In Scotland, only convicted criminals have their DNA profile stored on the DNA database. The profile contains details about individuals, which can be used for investigating crimes.

- If the whole adult population had their DNA profiles on the database, this would help in the investigation and prosecution of crime.

- To expand the database to include the whole population would be very expensive.

- Most people would approve of a new law requiring all adults to give a sample of their DNA to help with prevention and detection of crime.

- Money and time would be saved if everyone's DNA profile was taken only once.

- If a person's DNA is found to be present at a crime scene they could be viewed as guilty without any other supporting evidence.

- Currently, there are not enough safeguards in place to ensure that there is no misuse of DNA information.

- DNA evidence is not foolproof and may lead to wrongful convictions.

- Ethnic minorities are more likely, at present, to be on the database than white people.

- DNA databases are only as reliable as those who handle them—there are many spelling errors and inaccuracies in the storage of information.

SOURCE 2

Ethnic Group	% of Ethnic Group on Database
White	9
Asian	13
Black	37

Part D Question 3 (continued)

Result of Opinion Poll Survey

Should there be a new law requiring everyone over 18 to give a sample of DNA?	
Yes – 66%	No – 33%

If you were to serve on a jury would you count DNA evidence as more or less important than other evidence?		
More important – 65%	Less important – 4%	Equally important – 28%

SOURCE 3

Viewpoints

The DNA database should contain profiles of the whole population. The current system is unfair. It would be fairer to include everybody, guilty or innocent. Having everyone on the database means there will be no discrimination against ethnic minorities. Civil liberties groups and representatives of the black community say that the existing database reinforces racial bias in the criminal justice system. DNA evidence will not be used in all cases, but will help the police convict the right person in the most serious of crimes.

Police Spokesperson

The DNA database should be kept for profiles of convicted criminals only. The Universal Declaration of Human Rights states that everyone has the right to protection of their privacy in their family or home life. To have everyone's DNA profile on the database would mean innocent people are having their rights abused. If two people meet on the street and shake hands their DNA is transferred. If one of these people then commits a crime, the DNA of the person he or she shook hands with could be found at the crime scene. DNA evidence is not the answer to solving the great majority of crimes.

Civil Rights Spokesperson

You must decide which option to recommend to the Scottish Government, **either** the DNA database should contain profiles of the whole population (**Option 1**) **or** the DNA database should contain profiles of convicted criminals only (**Option 2**).

(i)   Using Sources 1, 2 and 3 above, **which option would you choose**?

(ii)   Give reasons to **support** your choice.

(iii)   **Explain** why you did not make the other choice.

Your answer must be based on all three sources.   10

NOW GO TO SECTION 3 ON *PAGE FIFTEEN*

MARKS | DO NOT WRITE IN THIS MARGIN

SECTION 3 — INTERNATIONAL ISSUES — 20 marks

Attempt ONE part, either

Part E—World Powers   on pages 15–17

OR

Part F—World Issues   on pages 18–20

PART E — WORLD POWERS

In your answers to Questions 1 and 2 you should give recent examples from a world power you have studied.

Question 1

All governments have different political institutions.

Describe, **in detail**, at least two main political institutions of the government of a world power you have studied.   **6**

Question 2

Social problems faced by world powers:

Poor education	Health inequalities	Fear of crime	Poor housing

Choose **one** of the social problems shown above.

Explain, **in detail,** why this issue continues to be a problem in a world power you have studied.   **6**

Part E (continued)

MARKS

Question 3

Study Sources 1, 2 and 3 below, then attempt the question which follows.

SOURCE 1

Life in the G20 country

This G20 state is a very large country with the world's biggest population of around 1.3 billion people. It is made up of a variety of different regions and ethnic groups. The largest ethnic group, by far, is the Han whose language remains the most common language throughout most of the country. Population and language spoken varies across the nation. There are 29 provinces and the part of the country where a person lives can have a major effect upon his or her life.

The average income is rising as the country becomes more prosperous. However, there are big differences in levels of income between different parts of the country, especially between rural and urban areas. Income differences are important because they have an effect upon success in education.

There are large differences in health and education between rural and urban areas. Urban areas tend to have better schools and health care. Since most of the wealthy people live in the cities they are able to afford the best in education and health. Rural areas are poorer and so too are education and health facilities.

Overall, the country is making very good progress and many people are becoming wealthy and enjoy a good standard of living. However, people in some parts enjoy a better life than people in other areas. Areas on the coast have benefited more from foreign investment. Coastal areas have more industry and tend to be better off with more manufacturing and service jobs and growing wealth.

SOURCE 2

Social and Economic Information about Life in Selected Regions

	Shanghai	Beijing	Beijing Guangdong	Yunnan	Guizhou	Tibet
Population	17.8 million	15.4 million	91.9 million	44.4 million	37.3 million	2.8 million
% Urban	89.0%	83.6%	60.7%	29.5%	26.9%	26.8%
% Rural	11.0%	16.4%	39.3%	70.5%	73.1%	73.4%
Life Expectancy (in years)	78	76	73	65	66	64
Percentage unable to read or write	5.9%	4.6%	7.6%	21.5%	19.7%	54.9%
Average Income per person (in Yuan)	46 718	32 061	17 213	5662	3603	6871

Part E Question 3 (continued)

MARKS

SOURCE 3

Information about Ethnic Composition in Selected Regions

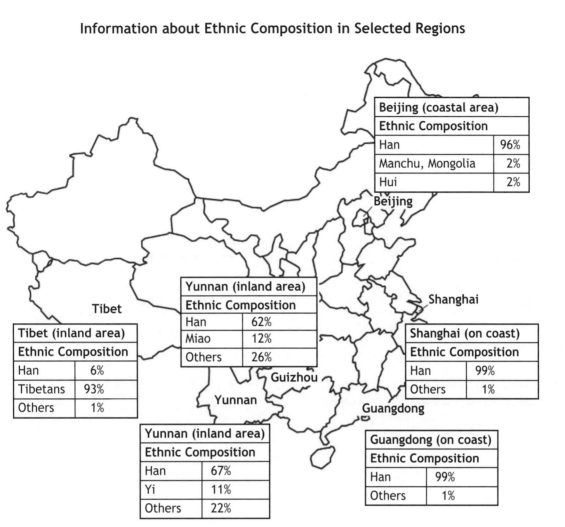

Beijing (coastal area)	
Ethnic Composition	
Han	96%
Manchu, Mongolia	2%
Hui	2%

Yunnan (inland area)	
Ethnic Composition	
Han	62%
Miao	12%
Others	26%

Tibet (inland area)	
Ethnic Composition	
Han	6%
Tibetans	93%
Others	1%

Shanghai (on coast)	
Ethnic Composition	
Han	99%
Others	1%

Yunnan (inland area)	
Ethnic Composition	
Han	67%
Yi	11%
Others	22%

Guangdong (on coast)	
Ethnic Composition	
Han	99%
Others	1%

Using Sources 1, 2 and 3 above, what **conclusions** can be drawn about life in the selected country?

You should reach a conclusion about each of the following:

- ethnic composition in different parts of the country

- the link between income and education

- health in urban and rural areas.

Your conclusions must be supported by evidence from all three sources. You should link information within and between sources in support of your conclusions.

Your answer must be based on all three sources.

8

PART F — WORLD ISSUES

In your answers to Questions 1 and 2 you should give recent examples from a world issue you have studied.

Question 1

> There are often a variety of factors which cause an international issue or problem.

Describe, **in detail**, at least two causes of an international issue or problem you have studied.

6

Question 2

International organisations which try to resolve international issues and problems		
NATO	European Union	African Union
United Nations Organisation	Charities and other NGOs	World Bank

Explain, **in detail**, why international organisations experience problems in trying to resolve an international issue you have studied.

6

Part F (continued)

MARKS

Question 3

Study Sources 1, 2, 3 and 4 below, then attempt the question which follows.

SOURCE 1

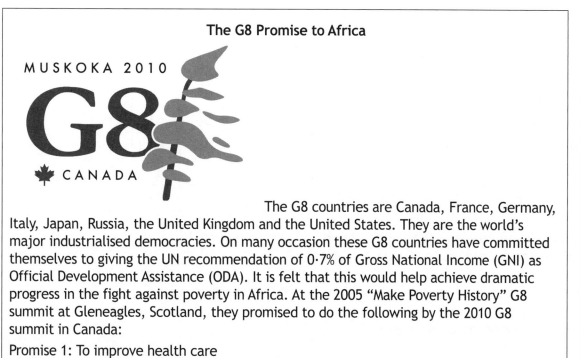

The G8 Promise to Africa

MUSKOKA 2010
G8
CANADA

The G8 countries are Canada, France, Germany, Italy, Japan, Russia, the United Kingdom and the United States. They are the world's major industrialised democracies. On many occasion these G8 countries have committed themselves to giving the UN recommendation of 0·7% of Gross National Income (GNI) as Official Development Assistance (ODA). It is felt that this would help achieve dramatic progress in the fight against poverty in Africa. At the 2005 "Make Poverty History" G8 summit at Gleneagles, Scotland, they promised to do the following by the 2010 G8 summit in Canada:

Promise 1: To improve health care

Promise 2: To more than double total ODA given to all less developed countries by 2010

Promise 3: To improve education

Promise 4: To deliver a $22·6 billion increase in ODA to Sub-Saharan Africa between 2005 and 2010

In terms of total ODA to all less developed countries, the G8 countries have all increased their contribution, with Canada almost doubling its ODA contribution. Recent health and education figures have been encouraging. Between 1996 and 2009 the % of HIV sufferers in Rwanda has declined from 7.0 % to 2.8%

SOURCE 2

Total ODA given by selected G8 countries to all less developed countries

Selected G8 Countries	2005		2007		2010	
	ODA $ Billions	% of GNI	ODA $ Billions	% of GNI	ODA $ Billions	% of GNI
Canada	2·6	0·27	4·1	0·29	5·1	0·33
France	8·5	0·41	9·9	0·38	12·9	0·50
Germany	7·5	0·28	12·3	0·37	12·7	0·38
Italy	2·5	0·15	4·0	0·19	3·1	0·15
Japan	8·9	0·19	7·7	0·17	11·0	0·20
United Kingdom	7·9	0·36	9·9	0·35	13·8	0·56
USA	19·7	0·17	21·8	0·19	30·0	0·21

Part F Question 3 (continued)

SOURCE 3

Health and Education Statistics

	Burundi		Ethiopia		Malawi	
	1996	2009	1996	2009	1996	2009
HIV % (age 15–49)	5·2	2·0	2·4	2·1	12·1	11·9
Infant Mortality Rate per 1000 Births	112	102	108	69	122	65
Life Expectancy at Birth (years)	45	51	49	56	52	53
% Primary School Completion	25	45	14	46	48	55
% Literacy Rate—females 15–24	48	75	28	40	65	85
% Literacy Rate—males 15–24	59	77	39	65	75	87

Using only the information in Sources 1, 2 and 3 above, what **conclusions** can be made about the G8 and aid to African countries?

You must make and justify conclusions about each of the headings below.

- The success of the G8 in meeting Promise 1.

- The success of the G8 in meeting Promise 2.

- The G8 country most committed to meet the UN aid recommendation.

8

Your conclusions must be supported by evidence from the sources. You should link information within and between the sources in support of your conclusions.

Your answer must be based on all three sources.

[END OF MODEL QUESTION PAPER]

2013 Model Paper 2

N5

National
Qualifications
MODEL PAPER 2

Modern Studies

Duration — 1 hour and 30 minutes

Total marks — 60

SECTION 1 — DEMOCRACY IN SCOTLAND AND THE UNITED KINGDOM — 20 marks

Attempt ONE part, EITHER

SECTION 2 — SOCIAL ISSUES IN THE UNITED KINGDOM — 20 marks

Attempt ONE part, EITHER

SECTION 3 — INTERNATIONAL ISSUES — 20 marks

Attempt ONE part, EITHER

Before attempting the questions you must check that your answer booklet is for the same subject and level as this question paper.

Read the questions carefully.

On the answer booklet, you must clearly identify the question number you are attempting.

Use **blue** or **black** ink.

Before leaving the examination room you must give your answer booklet to the Invigilator. If you do not, you may lose all the marks for this paper.

MARKS

SECTION 1 — DEMOCRACY IN SCOTLAND AND THE UNITED KINGDOM — 20 marks

Attempt ONE part, either

Part A — Democracy in Scotland　　　　on pages 2–6

OR

Part B — Democracy in the United Kingdom　　on pages 7–9

Part A — Democracy in Scotland

In your answers to Questions 1 and 2 you should give recent examples from Scotland.

Question 1

> The Scottish Parliament can make decisions about devolved matters for Scotland.

Describe, **in detail**, **two** devolved matters which the Scottish Parliament can make decisions about for Scotland.

4

Question 2

> Local councils in Scotland can raise money in different ways.

Explain, **in detail**, at least two ways in which local councils in Scotland can raise money.

6

NOW ATTEMPT QUESTION 3

Part A (continued)   MARKS

Question 3

Study Sources 1, 2 and 3 below, then attempt the question which follows.

You have been asked to recommend who should be your party's candidate in the local Council elections.

Option 1	Option 2
Candidate Ian McKay	Candidate Sally Anderson

SOURCE 1

SELECTED FACTS ABOUT INVERDON

Inverdon is a Council area in the North East of Scotland. It has a population of 263,000 which has significantly grown in recent years due to an inflow of migrant workers mainly from Eastern Europe. They have been useful to local business as they often find work on farms and in other low paid jobs. Unemployment amongst this group of migrant workers is very low.

Like all Scottish local authorities, Inverdon Council has been facing great financial difficulties in recent years. This has been due to less money coming from the Scottish Government to it and a decision to freeze the level of Council Tax paid by residents.

Selected Economic Statistics			
	Inverdon	Glasgow	Scotland
Average Weekly Pay	£450	£475	£455
Unemployment	4·2%	5·9%	4·0%

Selected Housing Statistics about Inverdon			
	2009	2010	2011
Average House Price (£000s)	210	185	200
Houses Built	2105	1226	950

Part A Question 3 (continued)

SOURCE 2

INVERDON DUNES GOLF DEVELOPMENT

Golf Development Company	Save Our Dunes Campaign
A large American company is seeking planning permission for a massive £750 million development. It will consist of two golf courses, a large 400-bed hotel and leisure complex, and 200 holiday homes for short-term rental.	A local pressure group has been set up to oppose the golf development. They have a number of concerns.
There will also be accommodation for 400 staff. A separate housing development nearby will make 300 homes available for sale, with prices starting at £600,000 per house.	They believe that the 4000-year-old dune system will be destroyed whilst 6 holes of the new golf course will be built on a Site of Special Scientific Interest which is protected by current law.
It is expected that the development will be a big boost to the local economy, as it will provide 5000 temporary construction jobs and 1250 permanent jobs. It is estimated that it will attract over 100,000 "golf tourists" from all over the world each year.	They are also of the opinion that roads will become busier leading to more congestion and air pollution.
	It is estimated that about 25,000 tourists already visit the area annually to enjoy the unspoilt views, the rare plants and animal species on the dunes. They believe that these visitors will no longer come.

SOURCE 3

Survey of Public Opinion in Inverdon

	Yes	No	Don't Know
Do you support the Inverdon Dunes Golf Development?	65%	25%	10%
Do you think that Inverdon Council is doing a good job?	35%	43%	22%
Do you think that Inverdon needs more migrant workers?	32%	55%	13%

Part A Question 3 (continued)

MARKS

INFORMATION ABOUT THE TWO CANDIDATES

Ian McKay

- I support the golf development. If elected, I will always welcome employment opportunities, and this development will provide lots of jobs for the area.

- The number of houses built in the area has grown steadily each year and I believe this is good for the town.

- I agree with the view of most local people that Inverdon Council is doing a good job for those who live in the area even though it faces financial difficulties.

- I am concerned about the number of migrant workers coming to Inverdon, and most local people share this view.

- Although wildlife tourists may be lost to the area, many more golf tourists will be attracted by the golf development.

Sally Anderson

- I am against the golf development because I believe that part of the course, if built according to plan, would be against the law.

- It is also clear that the vast majority of the public agree with my view that the golf development should not go ahead.

- Membership of the European Union allows people to travel to find work, and I think that migrant workers should be encouraged as they help our local economy.

- There are 300 homes to be built, but they are about 3 times more expensive than the average house in Inverdon, and few people will be able to afford them.

- Inverdon is a wealthy area, where people earn more than the Scottish average. I would much rather save our wild places than accept the jobs created by the golf development.

Part A Question 3 (continued)

You must decide which option to recommend, **either** Ian McKay as the candidate (Option 1) or Sally Anderson as the candidate (Option 2).

(i)   Using Sources 1, 2 and 3 above, **which option would you choose?**

(ii)   Give reasons to support your choice.

(iii)   Explain why you did not choose the other option.

Your answer must be based on all three sources.

10

NOW GO TO SECTION 2 ON *PAGE NINE*

PART B—DEMOCRACY IN THE UNITED KINGDOM

MARKS

In your answers to Questions 1 and 2 you should give recent examples from the United Kingdom.

Question 1

> Political Parties campaign to get their candidates elected as MPs.

Describe, **in detail**, **two** ways in which political parties campaign to get their candidates elected as MPs.

4

Question 2

> Some people want changes made to the House of Lords.

Explain, **in detail**, why some people want changes made to the House of Lords.

6

Part B (continued)

MARKS

Question 3

Study the Sources 1, 2 and 3 below, then attempt the question which follows.

You have been asked to recommend who should be your party's candidate for the constituency of Gleninch.

Option 1	Option 2
Kirsty Reid	Robbie McKay

SOURCE 1

BACKGROUND INFORMATION ABOUT GLENINCH CONSTITUENCY

- Gleninch is a constituency in the north of Scotland with a population of 35,265 people. It is a largely rural area with only one town, Inverinch, and a large number of scattered villages. The traditional industries of farming and fishing have been in decline in recent years. The unemployment rate is well above the national average.
- Many young people leave the area, moving to the big cities throughout the UK to look for jobs or to attend college or university.
- Tourism is very important to the local economy, with a lot of people employed in hotels, bed and breakfast accommodation and restaurants. Tourists tend to visit the area for a few days on short breaks, attracted by rare wildlife and spectacular, unspoilt scenery. However, there are a number of transport problems in the constituency, including high petrol prices and poor public transport.
- There is a proposal to build a wind farm in the area. This would involve the construction of 6 large wind turbines along the coast, as well as a 15-mile long power line built on tall pylons to take electricity to the rest of the country. This would create a few temporary construction jobs but will disturb local wildlife and impact on the scenery of the area.
- An American mining company wants to build a huge "super quarry" into a mountainside near Gleninch. This will produce crushed rock to build roads, railways and houses throughout the UK. The new quarry will create 150 new jobs in Gleninch.
- At the last General Election, the constituency was won by the Labour Party with a majority of just over 1000 votes. The Liberal Democrats came second. They are convinced that, with the right candidate, they can win the seat at the next election.

A Statistical Profile of Gleninch Constituency (2013)

	Gleninch	Comparison with Scottish Average
Average Income	£21185	-14%
Income Support claimants	15.1%	+22%
Unemployment Rate	5.6%	+13%
School leavers with no qualifications	3.6%	-33%
School leavers with Highers	58.6%	+13%
Serious Assaults	8.8 (per 10 000 people)	-73%
Housebreaking	3.8 (per 10 000 people)	-93%
Road Accidents	57 casualties	-44%

Part B Question 3 (continued)

MARKS

Survey of Local Liberal Democrat Members Question: *How important are these issues to people in the area?*				
Issue	Unimportant	Not Very Important	Fairly Important	Very Important
Environment	5%	25%	40%	30%
Health	2%	10%	53%	35%
Jobs	0%	0%	48%	52%
Women in Parliament	15%	52%	22%	11%

SOURCE 2

EXTRACT FROM CAMPAIGN SPEECH BY KIRSTY REID

- I support the proposed wind farm as it will provide many local jobs and help the local environment.

- Our local schools provide an excellent education. If selected, I will work to ensure this continues.

- Women make up over half the country's population and yet there are still very few of us who are MPs. This is a major priority for local party members and is an important reason why I should be the candidate.

- The local economy has been in decline recently. We need more jobs to keep our young people in the area. The new quarry will help with this, and I will work hard to see that it is allowed to go ahead.

- To attract more people to the area we need to improve transport links. I will make this a priority.

SOURCE 3

EXTRACT FROM CAMPAIGN SPEECH BY ROBBIE McKAY

- Tourism is very important to the area and so I will oppose the new wind farm as it will be an ugly blot on the landscape and deter tourists.

- Crime in Gleninch is among the worst in Scotland. I will campaign to improve policing in the area.

- Although new jobs are important, local Liberal Democrats are much more concerned about the environment. The new quarry will put more heavy lorries on our roads which are already more dangerous than the rest of the country. I will oppose it going ahead.

- The issue of health will be one of my main concerns, just as it is for local party members.

- Compared to the rest of the country, the people of Gleninch are not well off. I will do all I can to improve this.

You must decide which option to recommend, **either** Kirsty Reid as the candidate **(Option 1)** or Robbie McKay as the candidate **(Option 2)**.

(i)   Using Sources 1, 2 and 3 above and opposite, **which option would you choose**?

(ii)   Give reasons to support your choice.

(iii)   Explain why you did not choose the other option.

Your answer must be based on all three sources.

10

NOW GO TO SECTION 2 ON *PAGE NINE*

SECTION 2 — SOCIAL ISSUES IN THE UNITED KINGDOM — 20 marks

MARKS

Attempt ONE part, either

Part C — Social Inequality   on pages 10–12

OR

Part D — Crime and the Law   on pages 13–15

PART C – SOCIAL INEQUALITY

In your answers to Questions 1 and 2 you should give recent examples from the United Kingdom.

Question 1

The Government provides a range of financial benefits to help people in need.

Describe, **in detail**, at least two financial benefits provided by the Government which help people in need.

6

Question 2

Health inequalities continue to exist in the UK.

Explain, **in detail**, why health inequalities continue to exist in the UK.

6

Part C (continued)

MARKS | DO NOT WRITE IN THIS MARGIN

Question 3

Study Sources 1, 2 and 3 below, then attempt the question which follows.

SOURCE 1

Families in Britain have changed over the years. More than 4 in 10 people over the age of 16 in the UK are married. In 2005, the average age for first marriage was 31 for men and 29 for women. This had been 26 and 23 for men and women respectively 40 years earlier. In 2005, the average age for divorce was 43 for men and 40 for women. This had been 39 and 37 for men and women respectively in 1995.

Marriages and Divorces in Britain

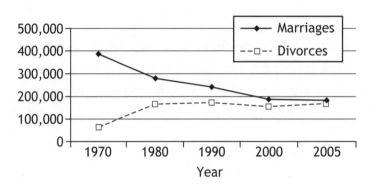

SOURCE 2

The total number of families reached 17 million in 2009. The "traditional" type of family has always been seen as a couple with dependent children. As the table shows, the percentage of families of each type in Britain has been changing. This may well have an impact on the welfare of dependent children. White people in Britain have the lowest percentage of married couples.

People in each type of household (%)

	1971	1981	1991	2009
One person	6	8	11	15
Couple no children	19	20	23	26
Couple with dependent children	52	47	41	35
Couple with non-dependent children only	10	10	11	9
Lone parent family	4	6	10	13
Other households	9	9	4	2

Part C Question 3 (continued)

MARKS

SOURCE 3

Some 9% of people in Britain are non-white. Ethnic groups differ in terms of family size and type. 62% of white families are married couples, 13% are cohabiting couples and 25% are lone parent families. From 1970 to 2005 there has been a large drop in marriages in general but not in divorces.

Using Sources 1, 2 and 3 above, what **conclusions** can be drawn about family life in the UK?

You should reach a conclusion about each of the following:

- changes in marriage and divorce in Britain

- the link between changes in marriages and changes in the "traditional" family

- the main difference between ethnic minority families and white families.

Your conclusion must be supported by evidence from the sources. You should link information within and between sources in support of your conclusions.

Your answer must be based on all three sources.

8

PART D - CRIME AND THE LAW

MARKS

DO NOT WRITE IN THIS MARGIN

In your answers to Questions 1 and 2 you should give recent examples from the United Kingdom.

Question 1

Scotland has its own system of adult courts.

Describe, **in detail**, at least two adult courts in Scotland.

6

Question 2

The use of the prison system has been criticised in recent years.

Explain, **in detail**, why the use of the prison system has been criticised in recent years.

6

MARKS | DO NOT WRITE IN THIS MARGIN

Part D (continued)

Question 3

Study Sources 1, 2 and 3 below and then attempt the question which follows.

SOURCE 1

The Scottish Government is considering a petition which would mean that any person carrying a knife would be given a mandatory custodial sentence. This would mean that possession of such a weapon would automatically result in the offender being sent to prison or a detention centre. Community groups have called on the Government to take action to deter young people from carrying knives. Many members of the public believe that people should automatically be sent to jail which would reduce crime – very few people think a fine would work. 1200 offenders were sentenced for possession of a knife between 2004 and 2009, but only 314 were given custodial sentences. Scottish Prisons reported that as a result of overcrowding, offenders were not serving their full sentence and were being released early. Automatic sentences may make this problem worse. In 2009, one in five people convicted of carrying a knife in Edinburgh had previously been charged for a similar offence. Some young people carry a knife for their own self-defence as they are worried about their own personal safety when they go out. 30% of young people thought that introducing tougher sentences would reduce knife crime.

Judges in Scotland think that they should be able to consider the personal circumstances of each case before sentencing. A custodial sentence can have a huge impact on the future of young people convicted. The number of people sent to prison for carrying a knife in public fell to a five year low in 2008 because only one in three offenders were jailed. The threat of a custodial sentence may work as the number of murders with knives has decreased since 2003/2004.

SOURCE 2

Year	Total number of murders	Number of murders with knives
2003/2004	140	70
2004/2005	137	62
2005/2006	129	59
2006/2007	120	54
2007/2008	114	49

Results of Public Opinion Survey on Methods to Reduce Knife Crime

Automatic Jail Sentence	67%
Community Service	29%
Fine	4%

Part D Question 3 (continued)

MARKS

SOURCE 3

View of Maureen Andrew

We need to tackle knife crime which is a problem in many of our communities. People in my area are extremely worried and they are demanding that the penalties for carrying knives are much tougher. Many people won't leave their houses because they are frightened of young people roaming around in gangs. Many youths have stated that carrying a knife is part of being in a gang and they have to be seen to be armed – peer pressure is a key factor. We must send out a strong message to troublemakers who go out looking for a fight. Many of these individuals have been charged before but this has had little effect on their behaviour. Young people have admitted that a jail sentence would make them think twice about carrying a knife.

Using Sources 1, 2 and 3 above, what **conclusions** can be drawn about knife crime in the UK?

You should reach a conclusion about each of the following:

- the rate of murders with knives

- reasons young people carry knives

- methods to reduce knife crime.

Your conclusions must be supported by evidence from the sources. You should link information within and between sources in support of your conclusions.

Your answer must be based on all three sources.

8

NOW GO TO SECTION 3 ON *PAGE FIFTEEN*

SECTION 3 — INTERNATIONAL ISSUES — 20 marks

Attempt ONE part, either

Part E—World Powers   on pages 16–18

OR

Part F—World Issues   on pages 19–22

PART E - WORLD POWERS

In your answers to Questions 1 and 2 you should give recent examples from a world power you have studied.

Question 1

> All governments respond to social and economic problems.

Describe, **in detail,** from a world power you have studied, at least two government's responses to social and economic problems.

6

Question 2

> Some citizens criticise their government for the limitations placed on their political rights.

Explain, **in detail**, why some citizens from a world power you have studied may criticise their government for the limitations placed on their political rights.

6

Part E (continued)

Question 3

Study Sources 1, 2 and 3 below and then attempt the question which follows.

SOURCE 1

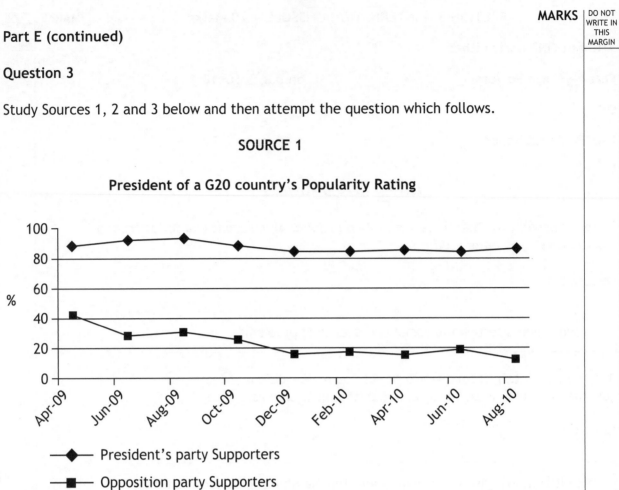

President of a G20 country's Popularity Rating

President's party Supporters

Opposition party Supporters

SOURCE 2

State	Question 1: For which party will you vote in the 2016 election? (%)		Question 2: At present, how good a job do you think the President is doing? (%)	
	President's Party	Opposition	A good job	A bad job
Alabama	45·9	39·5	49·1	42·9
Alaska	48·6	33·3	46·0	42·7
Hawaii	27·6	54·1	70·8	22·1
Idaho	49·7	34·6	46·3	43·7
Massachusetts	27·9	56·8	66·8	26·3
Rhode Island	24·5	56·2	66·6	26·3
Utah	51·9	31·0	47·8	40·8
Vermont	28·5	55·4	66·7	24·4
Wyoming	53·8	32·2	44·6	45·0

Part E Question 3 (continued)

SOURCE 3

The ethnic divide in the President's popularity

As the President seeks re-election, a recent newspaper poll measured public opinion on the three main issues of the Economy, Terrorism and Health. On the economy, 55% of Whites said they approved of the President's performance. Among Blacks, the figure was 91%. Thirty-six percent of Whites disapproved of the President's economic performance, while 2% of Blacks disapproved. Among Hispanics, 82% approved whilst the percentage of those disapproving was 10%. When asked if they were confident that the President could handle another major crisis, the different ethnic groups were also split. Fifty-five percent of Whites said they were confident, while 92% of Blacks said so. The Hispanic figure was 83%. When it came to the President's health reforms, the percentage of Whites in favour was 40%, whilst for Blacks it was 90% and 85% for Hispanics. Overall, nine out of ten Black and Hispanic Americans felt that the President cared about them while just over half of Whites shared this view. On each issue, a number of respondents had no view on the President's performance.

Using Sources 1, 2 and 3 explain why the view of Brad Simpson is **selective in the use of facts.**

The President remains popular, especially on the main issues for all ethnic groups and he remains popular especially amongst his own party.

View of Brad Simpson

In your answer you must:

give evidence from the sources that support Brad Simpson's view

and

give evidence from the sources that opposes Brad Simpson's view

Your answer must be based on all three sources.

8

PART F — WORLD ISSUES

MARKS | DO NOT WRITE IN THIS MARGIN

In your answers to Questions 1 and 2 you should give recent examples from a world issue you have studied.

Question 1

International issues have many consequences.

Describe, **in detail,** at least two consequences of an international issue you have studied.

6

Question 2

International organisations work hard to try to resolve international issues or problems.

Explain, **in detail**, at least two ways in which international organisations try to resolve an international issue or problem you have studied.

6

MARKS | DO NOT WRITE IN THIS MARGIN

Part F (continued)

Question 3

Study Sources 1, 2 and 3 below, then attempt the question which follows.

SOURCE 1

Adults (15–49) living with HIV/Aids (%)

African country	2003	2008
Botswana	23·6	23·9
Ethiopia	4·3	2·1
Lesotho	23·5	23·2
Swaziland	32·5	26·1
Zimbabwe	22·1	15·3

Population living in poverty (%)

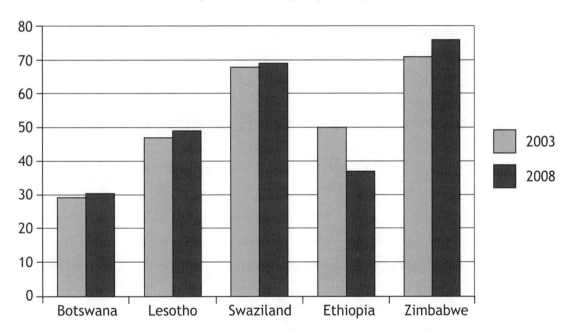

Part F Question 3 (continued)

MARKS | DO NOT WRITE IN THIS MARGIN

SOURCE 2

Education—How well is Africa shaping up?

UNESCO is promising to help African countries through its "Literacy Decade" campaign. However, it points out that Africa has a long way to go, as one fifth of African adults are illiterate.

The economic crisis in Zimbabwe has had an effect on the education budget in recent years. They cannot find enough qualified teachers to work in their schools.

The government of Lesotho has shown a commitment to education. They spent 13% of their GDP on schooling in 2008 whilst, in 2003, it was 11%. This has had a positive effect on literacy rates.

In Botswana, literacy rates have changed from 80% to 84% since 2003. Every child in Botswana can expect to go to school for twelve years. Swaziland, a country badly affected by HIV/Aids, has seen literacy rates go from 74% in 2003 to 81% in 2008. The situation in Ethiopia mirrors much of Africa with literacy levels going up although they are still low when compared to developed countries.

SOURCE 3

Total Foreign Debt (Millions of US Dollars)

African country	2003	2008
Botswana	392	422
Ethiopia	4400	3100
Lesotho	507	619
Swaziland	357	554
Zimbabwe	3400	5300

Total Aid received (Millions of US Dollars)

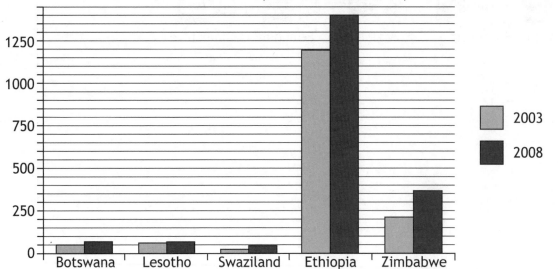

Part F Question 3 (continued)

MARKS

Using Sources 1, 2 and 3 explain, in detail, why the view of Diane Lochrie is **selective in the use of facts.**

> It is obvious that increasing aid reduces poverty in African countries and improves education, while those countries with increasing debt are unable to reduce the problem of HIV/AIDS.
>
> **View of Diane Lochrie**

In your answer you must:

give evidence from the sources that support Diane Lochrie's view

and

give evidence from the sources that opposes Diane Lochrie's view

Your answer must be based on all three sources.

8

[END OF MODEL QUESTION PAPER]

2013 Model Paper 3

**National
Qualifications
MODEL PAPER 3**

Modern Studies

Duration — 1 hour and 30 minutes

Total marks — 60

SECTION 1 — DEMOCRACY IN SCOTLAND AND THE UNITED KINGDOM — 20 marks

Attempt ONE part, EITHER

SECTION 2 — SOCIAL ISSUES IN THE UNITED KINGDOM — 20 marks

Attempt ONE part, EITHER

SECTION 3 — INTERNATIONAL ISSUES — 20 marks

Attempt ONE part, EITHER

Before attempting the questions you must check that your answer booklet is for the same subject and level as this question paper.

Read the questions carefully.

On the answer booklet, you must clearly identify the question number you are attempting.

Use **blue** or **black** ink.

Before leaving the examination room you must give your answer booklet to the Invigilator. If you do not, you may lose all the marks for this paper.

MARKS | DO NOT WRITE IN THIS MARGIN

SECTION 1 — DEMOCRACY IN SCOTLAND AND THE UNITED KINGDOM — 20 marks

Attempt ONE part, either

Part A — Democracy in Scotland   on pages 2–4

OR

Part B — Democracy in the United Kingdom   on pages 5–7

Part A - Democracy in Scotland

In your answers to Questions 1 and 2 you should give recent examples from Scotland.

Question 1

> The First Minister has many powers in the Scottish Government.

Describe, **in detail,** at least two powers of the First Minister in the Scottish Government.   **6**

Question 2

> Since the Scottish Parliament Election in 2011, Scotland has been governed by a majority government.

Explain, **in detail**, why some people believe majority government works well AND explain, **in detail**, why some people believe majority government does not work well.   **6**

NOW ATTEMPT QUESTIONS 3, 4 AND 5

Part A (continued)

MARKS | DO NOT WRITE IN THIS MARGIN

Question 3

Study **Sources 1**, **2 and 3**, then attempt the question which follows.

SOURCE 1

Road Bridge Tolls Campaign

Following the Scottish Parliament election in May 2007, the Scottish National Party Government announced that it would abolish tolls on both the Forth and Tay Road Bridges. This announcement followed a long campaign led by a pressure group called the National Alliance Against Tolls (NAAT).

NAAT members took part in a campaign to have the bridge tolls removed. They lobbied local councillors, MSPs and MPs. NAAT also lobbied political parties and persuaded the Liberal Democrats to support the scrapping of bridge tolls. Members wrote hundreds of letters to newspapers; the group set up its own website; they used the 10 Downing Street e-petition set up by the Prime Minister and asked supporters to add their names. A by-election in Dunfermline, caused by the death of the Labour MP, was an opportunity for the group to increase their support and gain publicity when they put forward a candidate.

One newspaper, the Dundee Courier, strongly supported the campaign to abolish the tolls while another, The Herald, was not in favour of ending tolls on the bridges. Trade Unions were concerned about the impact on their members. Some local residents and the Green Party were worried about the increase in traffic and the impact upon the environment if tolls were scrapped. Many business groups, however, thought that the ending of tolls would benefit the economy of Scotland.

SOURCE 2

Result of Dunfermline & West Fife By-Election

Party	Candidate	Votes	%
Liberal Democrats	William Rennie	12,391	35.83%
Labour	Catherine Stihler	10,591	30.63%
Scottish National Party	Douglas Chapman	7,261	21.00%
Conservative & Unionist	Dr Carrie Ruxton	2,702	7.81%
Scottish Socialist Party	John McAllion	537	1.55%
Scottish Christian Party	Rev George Hargreaves	411	1.19%
Abolish Forth Bridge Tolls Party	Tom Minogue	374	1.08%
UKIP	Ian Borland	208	0.60%
Common Good	Rev Dr Dick Rogers	108	0.30%

Part A Question 3 (continued)   MARKS | DO NOT WRITE IN THIS MARGIN

SOURCE 3

Selected Views on Bridge Tolls Campaign

Extracts from Statement by Tom Minogue (anti-toll by-election candidate):
Thank you to the people who voted for me . . . I consider that, taking all things into account, we have done well to poll 374 votes. It might not seem much but . . . this is no mean achievement when one considers that today marks the second week in existence for the Abolish Forth Bridge Tolls Party.

The NAAT website reported: for some reason, The Herald is still fighting to keep the tolls. This morning it published results of a poll of businesses, which included a question on removal of tolls. The result was that 58% of firms welcomed removal of tolls yet The Herald says—"*The result falls short of being a ringing endorsement of a significant policy initiative.*"

A Trade Union attacked the decision to scrap tolls on the Forth and Tay Bridges. The Transport and General Workers Union was concerned about job losses. It claimed the move will leave 175 of their members facing the loss of their jobs.

The Dundee Courier wrote: In the end it was all about people power. Tens of thousands of you backed The Courier's campaign to scrap tolls and make politicians act. It was a cause this paper believed could not be ignored and it was a cause our readers supported from the day we launched our campaign in March last year. By letter, phone or e-mail you said loud and clear "the tolls must go." Some 2000 of you added your signatures to the campaign in the first month, another 10,000 backed an online poll. Thousands more of you gave visible backing by displaying "Scrap The Tolls" stickers on your vehicles, taking the message with you wherever you travelled.

Using Sources 1, 2 and 3, explain why the view of Diana Jones is **selective in the use of facts.**

The campaign to end the tolls on the Forth and Tay Bridges was successful and had the support of the people of Scotland.

View of Diana Jones

In your answer you must:

give evidence from the sources that support Diana Jones' view

and

give evidence from the sources that opposes Diana Jones' view

Your answer must be based on all three sources.   8

NOW GO TO SECTION 2 ON *PAGE EIGHT*

PART B—DEMOCRACY IN THE UNITED KINGDOM

In your answers to Questions 1 and 2 you should give recent examples from the United Kingdom.

Question 1

> The Prime Minister has many powers in the UK Government.

Describe, **in detail**, at least two powers of the Prime Minister in the UK Government.

6

Question 2

> Since the UK General Election in 2010, the UK has been governed by a coalition government.

Explain, **in detail**, why some people believe coalition government works well AND explain, **in detail**, why some people believe coalition government does not work well.

6

Part B (continued)

MARKS | DO NOT WRITE IN THIS MARGIN

Question 3

Study Sources 1, 2 and 3 below, then attempt the question which follows.

SOURCE 1

Compulsory Voting

Election turnout has been falling in recent years and fewer people believe they have a duty to vote, leading to worries about the future of democracy in Britain. The Government is considering various ways to increase the number of people voting in elections. In the most recent UK General Election in 2010, turnout was 65%. This was a clear increase from the record low figure of 59.4% in 2001.

One suggestion has been to make voting compulsory. In the UK, compulsory voting is not part of electoral law. In a number of countries including Australia, Belgium, Greece and Brazil, voting is compulsory. Non-voters face a mixture of penalties, mainly fines. In Greece, turnout in elections is about 75% while in Australia in recent elections 95.4% of the electorate voted and of them, 4.8% spoiled their ballot paper.

Supporters of compulsory voting claim it increases turnout and so makes elections more democratic and representative of the views of voters. Parties do not have to worry about getting their supporters to vote and so can concentrate on the issues, leading to a better political debate.

Opponents of compulsory voting argue that having the right to vote also means having the right not to vote and it would be against British traditions to force reluctant voters to cast a vote. It would be difficult to enforce this law and would be a considerable waste of police and court time.

SOURCE 2

Survey of Public Opinion about Voting

Do you support making voting in elections compulsory?	
Yes	47%
No	49%
Don't Know	4%

Percentage of people over 18 who would definitely vote in a General Election, by age group.

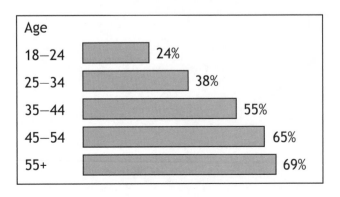

Part B Question 3 (continued)

MARKS

SOURCE 3

Selected Views on Compulsory Voting

- Brian Davidson MP said: "The introduction of compulsory voting is a way of getting people interested in politics, restoring a sense of community and confronting the issue of people who never vote."

- Oliver Heald MP said: "There is little support to make it a criminal offence not to vote . . . the police have better things to do. The challenge is for politicians to excite voters with their ideas."

- Forcing people to vote would not improve democracy in Britain. The reason why many people do not vote, especially young people, is that they do not think voting will make any difference and they do not have much trust in politicians. Forcing people into the polling booth would lead to a large number of spoiled ballot papers.

- Voting is a right and should be a duty. All citizens should participate in important decisions by voting. Ballot papers, however, should also have a space where voters can say "none of the above"; a high vote for none of the candidates will force politicians to pay more attention to the wishes of dissatisfied voters.

Using Sources 1, 2 and 3, explain why the view of Chris Knight is **selective in the use of facts.**

> **Compulsory voting would improve democracy and would be popular with voters.**
>
> **View of Chris Knight**

In your answer you must:

give evidence from the sources that support Chris Knight's view

and

give evidence from the sources that opposes Chris Knight's view

Your answer must be based on all three sources.

8

NOW GO TO SECTION 2 ON *PAGE EIGHT*

MARKS

SECTION 2 – SOCIAL ISSUES IN THE UNITED KINGDOM – 20 marks

Attempt ONE part, either

Part C – Social Inequality　　　　　　**on pages 8–12**

OR

Part D – Crime and the Law　　　　　　**on pages 13–16**

PART C - SOCIAL INEQUALITY

In your answers to Questions 1 and 2 you should give recent examples from the United Kingdom.

Question 1

> Living in poverty has a big effect on children.

Describe, **in detail**, **two** effects of living in poverty on children.　　　　**4**

Question 2

> Health in Scotland can be improved by government policies and individual action.

Explain, **in detail,** the ways in which health in Scotland can be improved by government policies **and** individual actions.　　　　**6**

Part C (continued)

MARKS

Question 3

Study the information in Sources 1, 2 and 3 below, then attempt the question which follows.

You are an adviser to the Scottish Government. You have been asked to recommend whether the Government should extend the scheme, which pays smokers to stop smoking, across the whole of Scotland, or to recommend scrapping the scheme.

Option 1	Option 2
Extend the scheme which pays smokers to stop smoking, across the whole of Scotland.	Scrap the scheme which pays smokers to stop smoking.

SOURCE 1

Facts and Viewpoints

The NHS in Dundee established a trial scheme in March 2009 which gives smokers financial incentives to give up cigarettes. The Scottish Government is considering whether to extend the scheme to the whole of Scotland.

Those on the scheme will have £12·50 credited onto an electronic card to buy groceries, if they pass a weekly breath test. The credits cannot be used to buy cigarettes or alcohol. Payments will be paid for a maximum of 12 weeks which will cost the NHS £150 per person.

There are 36,000 smokers in Dundee, about half of whom live in poverty. There are over 1 million smokers in Scotland, 43% of them live in poverty.

Some local people say it is unfair that smokers are getting extra money while others who live in poverty and don't smoke, get nothing.

It is hoped 1800 smokers will sign up for the project. The budget for the scheme is £540,000 over 2 years in Dundee. To extend the scheme across the whole of Scotland would cost £14 million.

Many NHS staff think that other methods such as nicotine gum are more effective in helping smokers to give up cigarettes.

After 3 months, 360 people had signed up to the project in Dundee.

The average cost to the NHS of nicotine replacements, such as patches and gum, is £800 per person.

Some experts believe that people need counselling to give up smoking.

Smoking-related illnesses cost the NHS in Scotland over £200 million per year.

Smokers spend an average of £51 per week on cigarettes. For those living in poverty, this is about 28% of their income.

Part C Question 3 (continued)

SOURCE 2

Success rate of selected help to stop smoking

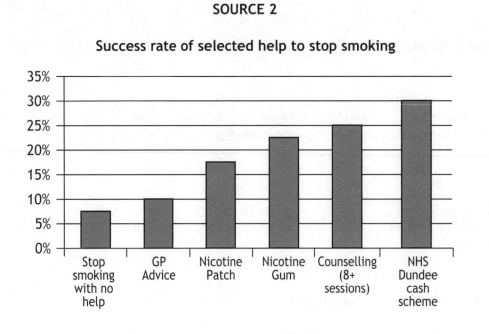

Percentage (%) success rate of counselling in stopping smoking

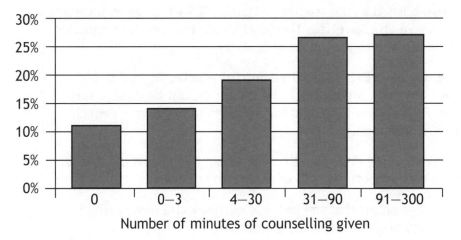

Number of minutes of counselling given

Part C Question 3 (continued)

SOURCE 3

Viewpoints

Giving up smoking is the single most important lifestyle decision that smokers can make to improve their health and standard of living. Giving grocery money to smokers to help them quit has worked in Dundee. An extra £12·50 per week will help some of the poorest families to buy healthy food which will also improve long-term health. Smoking-related illnesses cost the NHS millions of pounds every year and if we can get people to stop smoking using schemes like this, then it is money well worth spending. Those who quit will also save money every week through not buying cigarettes. This will make a huge difference to the income of families of ex-smokers.

Lewis McManus

Paying people to give up smoking will not work. It is unrealistic to expect people to give up for good after only 12 weeks. Alternatives such as nicotine gum and patches have proved to work in the long run. We should be encouraging people to go to long-term counselling which has proven to be a very effective method. Although the cost of alternatives may seem higher, it will save the NHS a huge amount of money in the long run. Many non-smoking families are living in poverty, but they are not being paid £12·50 extra a week to help with their shopping. This scheme may even encourage people to start smoking to get grocery money.

Maria Logan

You must decide which option to recommend to the Scottish Government: **either** to extend the scheme which pays smokers to stop smoking, across the whole of Scotland **(Option 1)**, **or** to scrap the scheme which pays smokers to stop smoking **(Option 2)**.

(i)   Using Sources 1, 2 and 3 above, **which option would you choose**?

(ii) Give reasons to **support** your choice.

(iii) **Explain** why you did not make the other choice.

Your answer must be based on all three sources.

10

NOW GO TO SECTION 3 ON *PAGE SIXTEEN*

PART D – CRIME AND THE LAW

In your answers to Questions 1 and 2 you should give recent examples from the United Kingdom.

Question 1

> The work of the police in Scotland involves a variety of roles.

Describe, **in detail,** two roles of the police in Scotland.   **4**

Question 2

> Scottish Courts often use alternative punishments to prison when dealing with offenders.

Explain, **in detail**, why Scottish Courts often use alternative punishments to prison when dealing with offenders.   **6**

Part D (continued)

Question 3

Study Sources 1, 2 and 3 below and opposite, then attempt the question which follows.

You are an adviser to the Scottish Government. You have been asked to recommend whether the police should install more CCTV cameras or should not install more CCTV cameras.

Option 1 Install more CCTV cameras.	**Option 2** Should not install more CCTV cameras.

SOURCE 1

Facts and Viewpoints

CCTV cameras were introduced to Scotland's streets as a method of tackling crime. There are now approximately 2,335 cameras in Scotland monitoring public spaces such as city centres, parks and shopping centres.

- CCTV is proven to be highly effective in reducing crime in some places eg hospitals and car parks.

- Some research indicates where cameras are installed crime increases in nearby areas without CCTV cameras.

- Police believe that criminals are more likely to plead guilty when presented with CCTV evidence. This saves time in court and up to £5,000 of the costs of a trial.

- A case study in the Greater Glasgow area could find no link between the installation of CCTV cameras and a reduction in crime.

- Police officers report that one of their big frustrations is broken and vandalised cameras and CCTV images which do not capture offences clearly enough.

- There were 3,318 recorded incidents in 2008/9 using CCTV cameras which resulted in 587 evidence discs being provided for the Procurator Fiscal Service.

- Many members of the public are concerned that more CCTV means a loss of civil liberties and an invasion of their private lives.

- The majority of the public believe that the installation of more CCTV cameras is a positive thing.

- Scotland's cities already have too many cameras in operation compared to other countries, costing a huge amount of money.

- Strathclyde Police recently claimed a 75% drop in anti-social behaviour following the installation of a £130,000 CCTV system in a town with a history of this type of problem.

Part D Question 3 (continued)

SOURCE 2

Statistics

Area

	Crimes per year before CCTV installed	Crimes per year after CCTV installed	Percentage change
City	1,526	1,098	−20%
City car park	794	214	−73%
Hospital	18	12	−33%
Inner city estate	160	182	+14%

Public feelings on installation of CCTV cameras

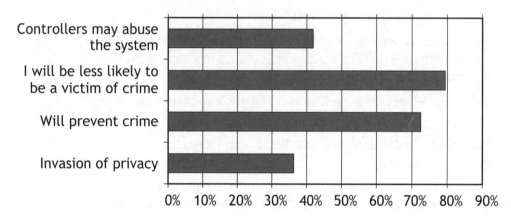

SOURCE 3

Viewpoints

Law abiding citizens have nothing to fear from CCTV; in fact it can help to protect them by deterring criminals from committing unlawful actions. CCTV can save taxpayers money by speeding up court cases. CCTV is of great benefit to police forces around the country especially when dealing with anti-social behaviour. The CCTV operators can direct the police to any possible flashpoints so that they can deal with problems before they arise. In addition, if a crime is committed, the CCTV evidence can be used in court to identify a criminal. We should use more new technology to aid the fight against crime.

John Morton

Installing CCTV cameras does not reduce crime rates. CCTV cameras are not effective in solving even straightforward crimes like street robberies. One problem is that some operators have not been trained in using the system properly and as a result, the cameras can be badly positioned and out of focus. CCTV is an invasion of privacy as most ordinary citizens do not commit crime but still have their movements followed and recorded up to 300 times per day. At best, CCTV only makes offenders move away from areas with cameras to commit crimes where there are none. Too much money is wasted on CCTV cameras; this money would be better spent putting more police on the street.

Pauline Clark

You must decide which option to recommend to the Scottish Government, **either** they should install more CCTV cameras (**Option 1**) **or** should not install more CCTV cameras (**Option 2**).

Using Sources 1, 2 and 3 above, **which option would you choose**?

(i)   Give reasons to **support** your choice.

(ii)   **Explain** why you did not make the other choice.

Your answer must be based on all three sources.   **10**

NOW GO TO SECTION 3 ON *PAGE SIXTEEN*

SECTION 3 — INTERNATIONAL ISSUES — 20 marks

Attempt ONE part, either

Part E—World Powers   on pages 17–20

OR

Part F—World Issues   on pages 21–24

PART E - WORLD POWERS

In your answers to Questions 1 and 2 you should give recent examples from a world power you have studied.

Question 1

Citizens have many rights and responsibilities.

Describe, **in detail**, the rights and responsibilities of citizens from a world power you have studied.

6

Question 2

Social Problems faced by World Powers

Some groups experience social and economic inequalities.

Explain, **in detail**, why some groups from a world power you have studied experience social and economic inequality.

6

Part E (continued)

Question 3

Study Sources 1, 2 and 3 below and then attempt the question which follows.

SOURCE 1

Progress made in tackling HIV/AIDS

This G20 African country still has one of the worst death rates from HIV/AIDS and has the largest number of HIV infected people in the world. At its peak in 2001 more than 20% of adults were infected with HIV and life expectancy fell from 60 years to 41 years. Since 2004, there has been a significant change in policies and programmes. On World AIDS Day, December 1, 2009, the President stated his intention to get an HIV test and encouraged all the country's people to learn about their HIV status. The Government announced an increase in budget support for HIV/AIDS in 2010 to pay for the additional patients who will qualify for treatment under the new guidelines. Although the Government has made good progress in the treatment of HIV/AIDS, there are still major challenges as not all citizens get access to HIV prevention and treatments.

Progress has been made in the treatment of women and children. According to a UN report, the number of pregnant women receiving antiretroviral treatment (ART), which prevents mother-to-child transmission of HIV, almost doubled between 2010 and 2012. It also noted that ART is now available to over half of those in need, although provincial differences remain.

The UN report found that the Government's plan to tackle HIV/AIDS is one of the largest treatment coverage programmes in the world. As the country is ranked second in the world in terms of domestic spending on AIDS programmes. However, although there are signs that the HIV/AIDS epidemic has stabilised, the number of adults with HIV/AIDS remains high. Some Provinces have experienced higher rates of HIV/AIDS compared to others and this has reduced life expectancy in some Provinces.

SOURCE 2

Provincial Health Data 2012

Province	Percentage of deaths due to AIDS	Life expectancy (in years)	Percentage of HIV prevalence among children
Eastern Cape	43·2%	46	2·5%
Free State	52·5%	47	3·1%
Gauteng	55·7%	50	3·1%
KwaZulu Natal	57·9%	47	3·4%
Limpopo	42·7%	45	2·7%
Mpumalanga	56·3%	46	4·5%
Northern Cape	35·9%	53	1·9%
North West	54·2%	46	2·6%
Western Cape	28·5%	55	0·9%
Whole Country	43·0%	49	2·5%

Part E Question 3 (continued)

Treatment Gap: number of people who need antiretroviral treatment (ART) and those who are receiving ART, by Province

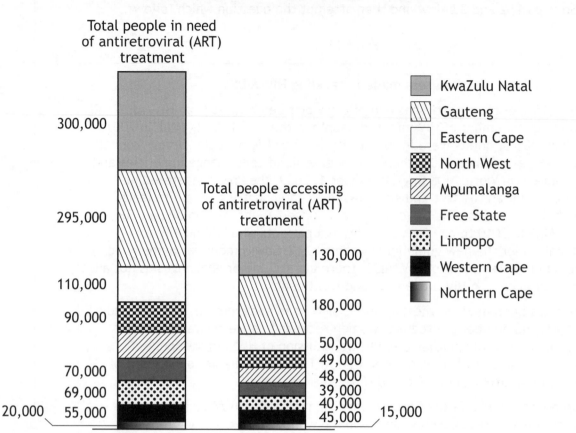

SOURCE 3

Year	Percentage of pregnant women who are HIV positive receiving antiretroviral (ART) treatment	Percentage of women attending antenatal clinics who are HIV positive
2004	15%	30%
2005	34%	30%
2006	52%	29%
2007	61%	28%
2008	73%	28%

MARKS

Part E Question 3 (continued)

Using Sources 1, 2 and 3 above, what **conclusions** can be drawn about HIV/AIDS in the country selected?

You should reach a conclusion about each of the following:

- HIV/AIDS in adults mothers and children

- provincial differences

- how effective the Government is in dealing with HIV/AIDS.

Your conclusions must be supported by evidence from the sources. You should link information within and between sources in support of your conclusions.

8

Your answer must be based on all three sources.

PART F — WORLD ISSUES

MARKS

In your answers to Questions 1 and 2 you should give recent examples from a world issue you have studied.

Question 1

The consequences of international issues impact on vulnerable groups.

Describe, **in detail**, at least two consequences of an international issue on vulnerable groups.

6

Question 2

International issues or problems are difficult to resolve.

Explain, **in detail**, why it is difficult to resolve an international issue or problem you have studied.

6

Part F (continued)

MARKS

Question 3

Study Sources 1, 2 and 3 below, then attempt the question which follows.

SOURCE 1

Terrorist activity around the world in 2012

The international community has had some success in recent years in the battle against terrorism. This has resulted in the number of terrorist related incidents worldwide dropping from a high in 2008 to a low in 2012. The amount of incidents in individual countries has also come down with the amount in Afghanistan decreasing. However, the number of terrorist incidents in Somalia and Spain has increased which is a worrying trend. In Somalia much has to be done to return the rule of law to society as the country is suffering from political and economic failure.

The motives for terrorist incidents varied from country to country. In Afghanistan, Pakistan and Somalia the most common motive for terror was religious reasons. This is due to Islamic extremism in these countries. In Spain nationalist reasons was the main motive. The amount of deaths caused by terrorism remains very high even although the amount of terrorist incidents has dropped. More people died in a terrorist incident in Afghanistan than anywhere else where as the USA was the safest place from terrorism. In Pakistan a high number of deaths were caused by suicide attacks and car bombings.

SOURCE 2

Number of terrorist incidents worldwide

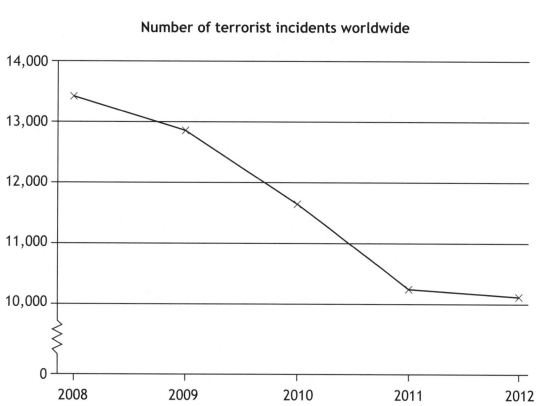

Part F (continued)

Terrorist incidents in selected countries 2010–2012

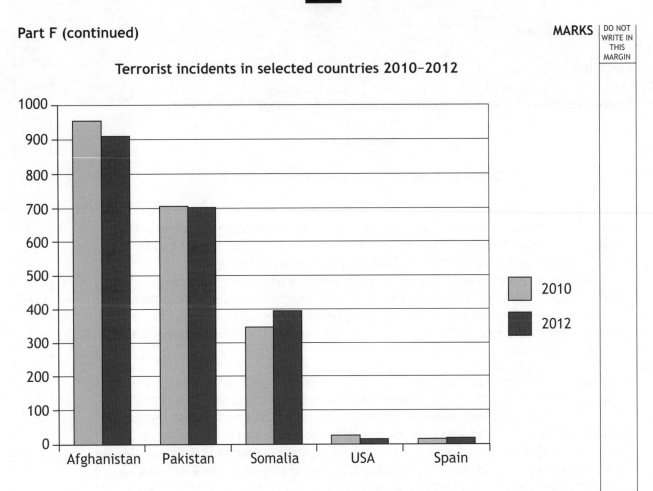

Part F (continued)

MARKS

DO NOT
WRITE IN
THIS
MARGIN

SOURCE 3

Motive for terrorist incidents 2012

	Religion	Nationalism	Political	Other
Afghanistan	546	179	156	31
Pakistan	478	102	98	23
Somalia	125	80	91	2
USA	4	1	5	2
Spain	4	11	2	1

Deaths caused by terrorist incidents 2012

Afghanistan	2193
Pakistan	1898
Somalia	1012
USA	8
Spain	11

Using sources 1, 2 and 3, what **conclusions** can be drawn about terrorism around the world?

You must reach a conclusion about each of the following:

- changes in the level of terrorist incidents worldwide

- motives behind terrorist incidents in selected countries

- the levels of terrorist incidents in selected countries.

Your conclusions must be supported by evidence from the sources. You should link information within and between sources in support of your conclusions.

Your answer must be based on all three sources.

10

[END OF MODEL QUESTION PAPER]

SQA AND HODDER GIBSON NATIONAL 5 MODERN STUDIES 2013

Section 1

Part A

1. *Candidates can be credited in a number of ways up to a maximum of 4 marks.*

   Possible approaches to answering the question:

   Pressure groups try to influence the Scottish Government by having a demonstration, lobbying, petitions and getting media attention.

   [2 marks awarded in total—list type answer]

   Trade Unions can try to influence the Government by going on strike, for example NHS doctors have threatened industrial action.

   [2 marks for a single point plus relevant example]

   Newspapers can try to influence the Government by printing stories that are very critical of the Government. Bad publicity can make the Government unpopular, for example when the Daily Record started a campaign against organised crime hoping that the Scottish Government and courts would clamp down.

   [3 marks for a developed point with exemplification]

   Reference to aspects of the following will be credited:

   ### Pressure Groups
   - Demonstrations/protest, eg recent protests by the SDL and UAF outside the Scottish Parliament.
   - Petitions—including e-petitions and submissions to the petitions committee.
   - Actions to attract media attention, eg campaign for safer cycle routes using celebrities such as Sir Chris Hoy in a mass cycle ride through Edinburgh.
   - Lobbying—contacting elected members of the Parliament to try to gain their support. This can be done by pressure groups themselves or they may employ advisors, ie professional lobbyists.
   - Direct action—disruptive and often illegal forms of protest, eg the Faslane peace camp.

   ### Trade Unions
   - Industrial action such as strikes, work to rule, overtime bans. This may be especially effective in the public sector, eg proposed action by NHS doctors.
   - Demonstrations/protest—recent demonstrations organised by teaching unions.
   - Petitions—including e-petitions and submissions to the petitions committee.
   - Actions to attract media attention, eg prison officers protesting outside their prisons.

   ### The Media
   - Newspapers supporting/opposing campaigns by pressure groups, eg recent highlighting of new medical tests introduced for disability benefits.
   - Newspapers supporting/opposing a particular political party during election campaigns, eg the changing support of the Sun newspaper in recent elections.
   - Newspapers highlighting what they see as Government incompetence/achievements, eg coverage of debate over continuation of universal benefits.
   - Broadcast media strictly controlled by legislation so it cannot attempt to influence the Government.

2. *Candidates can be credited in a number of ways up to a maximum of 8 marks.*

   Candidates who only explain either advantages or disadvantages should be awarded a maximum of six marks.

   Possible approaches to answering the question:

   An advantage of the Additional Member System is that it is a fairly proportional system.

   [1 mark]

   An advantage of AMS is that it provides better representation as it gives voters a choice of MSP to consult.

   [2 marks—developed point]

   An advantage of AMS is that it provides better representation as it gives voters a choice of MSP to consult. In any constituency you have a constituency and list MSPs.

   [3 marks—well developed point]

   An advantage of AMS is that it is a system where voters have two votes. One vote uses the First Past the Post system so you have a directly elected MSP for the constituency and the other vote uses the list system to elect regional MSPs. This means AMS provides the advantages of both systems.

   [4 marks—developed points with some detail and analysis]

   Reference to aspects of the following will be credited:

Advantages	Disadvantages
• More proportional—Scottish elections have had a closer correlation between votes and seats. • Retains elements of FPTP so some direct representation— voters in every constituency know who to contact. • Greater choice—each voter can contact a number of MSPs due to the regional list element. • Smaller parties can be successful, eg Greens in Scottish Parliament.	• Too many representatives—129 MSPs is seen by many as a "top heavy" system. • Representatives to Parliament elected under two different systems thus creating almost a "two tier" system of MSPs. • System more complex than FPTP so may be more difficult for many voters to understand. • Retention of FPTP element still allows some parties to dominate disproportionately, eg SNP dominating this ballot.

3. *Candidates can be credited in a number of ways up to a maximum of 8 marks.*

   Possible approaches to answering the question:

   The work done by committees
   Much of the important work of the Parliament is done in committees (Source 1).
   Committees on public audit, finance, justice etc (Source 2).

Hosted debates on knife crime (Source 3).

> [1 mark awarded overall—no conclusion reached or judgement made. A series of relevant points arranged under a correct heading.]

- Much of the important work of the Parliament done in committees (Source 1).
- Completed inquiries into a range of subjects (Source 1).
- Role of scrutinising the work of the Government and legislation (Source 1) link to paragraph 4 (Source 1).
- Can request debating time (Source 1) link with (Source 3) debate on cancer treatment drugs.
- Can introduce legislation—but only one in 2008-09 (Source 1).
- Source 2 indicates the range of areas of interest of Committees, eg Finance, Public Petitions, Justice (Source 2).
- 2008-09 Public Petition Committee—112 new petitions lodged; considered over 200 petitions (Source 3).
- Inquiry into availability of cancer treatment drugs (Source 3) link with (Source 1).
- Hosted debates on knife crime (Source 3).
- Possible conclusion—committees do a lot of work and play an important role in the work of the Scottish Parliament.

The membership of committees

The membership of the committees is made up of MSPs from every party. This is supported by evidence from Source 3 which says The Public Petitions Committee has 9 members; Labour 3, SNP 3, and one each from the Conservatives, Liberal Democrats and the Green Party. [2 marks. Conclusion given but taken from Source 1—supported by accurate and relevant evidence from Source 3.]

- MSPs from every party are members of the committees (Source 1).
- Committee Convenors, who chair meetings, drawn from different parties (Source 1) link with Source 2.
- Conveners drawn from Conservative, Labour, SNP, Liberal Democrats and Greens (Source 2).
- The Public Petitions Committee has 9 members; Labour 3, SNP 3, and one each from the Conservatives, Liberal Democrats and the Green Party (Source 3).
- Possible conclusion—all parties play a role in the Committees.

Public involvement in committees

Members of the public are able to get involved in politics through the committee system. [original conclusion] This conclusion is supported by evidence from Source 1 which says that committee meetings have been held around Scotland in places such as Fraserburgh, Ayr and Aberdeen. This is further supported in Source 3 which says that the Public Petitions Committee system gives members of the public direct access to policy development and also that members of the public have lodged over 1,244 petitions in the last 10 years.

> [3 marks awarded]

- Committee meetings have taken place in venues around Scotland, including Fraserburgh, Ayr and Aberdeen (Source 1).
- Most committees meet weekly or fortnightly in one of the Scottish Parliament's committee rooms—or in locations around Scotland (Source 1).
- Most meetings are open to the public (Source 1).
- The public petitions system provides members of the public with direct access to the policy development and scrutiny process (Source 3).

- The existence of the Public Petitions Committee means that petitioners can raise issues of concern directly with their Parliament (Source 3).
- The committee launched a year-long inquiry investigating ways to increase public awareness of, and participation in, the petitions process (Source 3).
- The e-petitions system, which allows petitions to be raised online, continued to be influential, with around two-thirds of petitions being lodged in this form (Source 3).
- 1,244 petitions have been lodged by members of the public over 10 years (Source 3).
- Possible conclusion—the committees are open to the public and the public can participate in a variety of ways.

Part B

1. *Candidates can be credited in a number of ways **up to a maximum of 4 marks**.*

Possible approaches to answering the question:

Pressure groups try to influence the UK Government by having a demonstration.

> [1 mark for an accurate but undeveloped point]

Trade Unions can try to influence the Government by going on strike, for example NHS doctors have threatened industrial action.

> [2 marks for a single point plus relevant example]

Newspapers can try to influence the Government by printing stories that are very critical of the Government. Bad publicity can make the Government unpopular, for example when some newspapers criticised the Government for trying to bring in the 'pasty tax' and the Government changed its mind.

> [3 marks for a developed point with exemplification]

Reference to aspects of the following will be credited:

Pressure Groups
- Demonstrations/protest, eg recent protests outside the House of Commons concerning student fees.
- Petitions—including e-petitions.
- Actions to attract media attention, eg Greenpeace campaign against whaling.
- Lobbying—contacting elected members of the parliament in order to try to gain their support. This can be done by pressure groups themselves or they may employ advisors, ie professional lobbyists. Also mass lobbying.
- Direct action—disruptive and often illegal forms of protest, eg the Faslane peace camp, hunt saboteurs, anti-abortion groups.

Trade Unions
- Industrial action such as strikes, work to rule, overtime bans. This may be especially effective in the public sector, eg strike action by NHS doctors.
- Demonstrations/protest—recent demonstrations organised by teaching unions.
- Petitions—including e-petitions.
- Actions to attract media attention, eg blockades of petrol depots.

The Media
- Newspapers supporting/opposing campaigns by pressure groups, eg support of some newspapers for a referendum over Europe.
- Newspapers supporting/opposing a particular political party during election campaigns, eg the traditional Labour versus Tory split in the press.

- Newspapers highlighting what they see as Government incompetence/achievements, eg Chief Whip incident with police officers.
- Broadcast media strictly controlled by legislation so cannot attempt to influence the Government.

2. *Candidates can be credited in a number of ways* **up to a maximum of 8 marks.**

Candidates who only explain either advantages or disadvantages should be awarded a maximum of six marks.

Possible approaches to answering the question:

An advantage of the First Past the Post system is that it is easy for voters to understand.

[1 mark]

An advantage of FPTP is that it provides a clear winner in each constituency as a simple majority is all that is needed.

[2 marks—developed point]

A disadvantage of FPTP is that many voters in safe seats feel that their vote is worthless. For example, a Labour supporter in a safe Conservative constituency may not bother voting as Labour have very little chance of winning in that seat.

[3 marks—well developed point]

A disadvantage of FPTP is that in safe constituencies the parties have a lot of power in choosing the MP. For example, in a safe Labour seat like Kirkcaldy and Cowdenbeath (Labour majority 23,000) it may not matter who the local Labour party chooses as their candidate as the party has such a large majority. Many voters always vote for the same party. This suggests that local party activists effectively choose the MP and not local voters. Marginal constituencies actually provide voters with more power, eg Edinburgh South which has a Labour majority of 300.

[4 marks—developed points with some detail, analysis and exemplification]

Reference to aspects of the following will be credited:

Advantages	Disadvantages
• Straightforward system means voters not confused which may make voters feel part of the democratic process and encourage participation. • Directly elected representative—one per constituency. MPs can be held directly accountable by constituents. • Usually a quick result is achieved which avoids the uncertainty of some PR systems. • Extremist parties such as the BNP have very little chance of gaining representation.	• Not proportional so many voters feel their votes are wasted, eg Labour supporter in a safe Conservative seat. • Encourages electorate to vote tactically. This adversely affects the democratic nature of the process. • Many MPs elected on a minority of the vote, ie winner takes all. • Possible for party to form majority government on minority of the popular vote.

3. *Candidates can be credited in a number of ways* **up to a maximum of 8 marks.**

Possible approaches to answering the question:

The work done by committees
Much of the important work of the Parliament is done in select committees (Source 1).

There are Select Committees on lots of issues (Source 2). Select Committees have the power to investigate what they want. (Source 3).

[1 mark awarded overall—no conclusion reached or judgement made. A series of relevant points arranged under a correct heading.]

- Some of the most important work of Parliament goes on in the many Select Committees (Source 1).
- Role is to "examine the expenditure, administration and policy of the principal Government departments" (Source 1).
- Over the years, the scrutiny role of the Select Committees has become well-established and well-publicised (Source 1).
- Committees play a central part in the work of the Parliament—taking evidence from witnesses including senior Government members, scrutinising legislation and conducting inquiries (Source 1).
- Source 2 indicates the range of areas of interest of Committees, eg Defence, Foreign Affairs, Treasury (Source 2).
- The Treasury Select Committee took a leading role in investigating the financial and banking crisis of 2008–09 (Source 3).
- The Committee chooses its own subjects of inquiry.
- Parliament has given the Committee the power to send for "persons, papers and records". It therefore has powers to insist upon the attendance of witnesses, such as ministers and civil servants, and the production of papers and other material (Source 3).
- Possible conclusion—Committees do a lot of work and play an important role in the work of the UK Parliament.

The membership of committees
The membership of the committees is made up of backbench MPs from every party. This is supported by evidence from Source 3 which says The Treasury Select Committee has 8 Labour members and two Liberal democrats.

[2 marks. Conclusion given taken from Source 1—supported by accurate and relevant evidence from Source 3.]

- Committees normally consist of backbench members (Source 1).
- Membership reflects the composition of the parties in the House of Commons as a whole. This means the governing party always has a majority (Source 1).
- Most committee reports are unanimous, reflecting a more non-party way of working. Different parties often work together and try to reach agreement in the committees (Source 1).
- MPs from every party take part in the work of the committees with Committee Chairs being drawn from different parties (Source 1).
- Chairs drawn from three parties, ie Labour, Conservative and Liberal Democrats (Source 2).
- The Treasury Select Committee has 14 members; Labour 8, Conservatives 4, Liberal Democrats 2 (Source 3).
- Possible conclusion—Committees are made up of all parties although governing party (Labour in 2008–09) has biggest role.

Public involvement in committees
Members of the public have several opportunities to get involved in politics through the select committee system. [original conclusion] This conclusion is supported by evidence from Source 1 which says that committee meetings have been held in different parts of the country with the public attending. The public are welcome to attend and can also feel involved through television coverage, internet broadcast

and the website. The public have been involved in recent Select Committee investigations, eg Fred Goodwin and the 10p tax issue. (Source 3)

- Select Committees can hold meetings in different parts of the country (Source 1).
- Members of the public can attend (Source 1).
- Each has its own website and committee meetings are broadcast on television and the Internet (Source 1).
- Members of the public are welcome to attend hearings of the committee (Source 3).
- At a televised hearing of the Treasury Select Committee, former Royal Bank of Scotland chief executive Sir Fred Goodwin told MPs he "could not be more sorry" for what had happened during the banking crisis (Source 3).
- Possible conclusion—public does have some access to work of committees.

Section 2
Part C

1. *Candidates can be credited in a number of ways **up to a maximum of 6 marks**.*

Possible approaches to answering the question:

The Government provides the pension for elderly people.
[1 mark—accurate but undeveloped point]

The Government tries to help unemployed people by providing "Jobcentre plus" which gives them free interview advice.
[2 marks—accurate point with development]

The Government has helped protect ethnic minority groups through the Equality Act (2010). This replaces various other laws against racism. These groups cannot be discriminated against in any walk of life, eg housing, employment, benefits, leisure, law and order.
[3 marks—accurate point with development and exemplification]

Ethnic minority groups
- Protection from discrimination through various pieces of legislation now consolidated by the Equality Act (2010).
- Support of various anti-racist campaigns, eg "One Scotland, Many Cultures".
- Various social benefits provided to all affected groups, eg Income Support, Housing Benefit. Welfare Reform Act introducing the Universal Benefit and reforming the Social Fund system.

Elderly people
- Protection from discrimination through various pieces of legislation now consolidated by the Equality Act (2010).
- Provision of the State Retirement Pension and introduction of new Workplace Pensions in 2012.
- Various social benefits provided to all affected groups, eg Income Support, Housing Benefit. Welfare Reform Act which makes big changes to Disability Living Allowance.
- Various free, universal benefits available to the elderly such as free personal care in Scotland and free bus travel.

Unemployed
- Various services provided by Jobcentre plus such as "The Work Programme", "Work Clubs", "Enterprise Clubs" etc. Jobcentre plus also provides advice, job search facilities and access to benefits.
- Provision of benefits including the new Universal Credit which aims to encourage claimants back into work. This will involve reform of the Employment and Support Allowance, Job Seekers Allowance etc.

- Training/retraining opportunities through further education and organisations such as "Skills Development Scotland" providing schemes like Modern Apprenticeships and its website "My world of work".

Lone parent families
- Protection from discrimination through the Equality Act (2010).
- Various social benefits provided to all affected groups, eg Income Support, Housing Benefit. Welfare Reform Act introducing the Universal Benefit which contains a childcare element replacing Child Tax Credit.
- Free nursery places for three and four year olds, Sure Start Children's Centres, Maternity Grants etc.

Disabled groups
- Protection from discrimination through the Equality Act (2010), replacing various pieces of disability rights legislation.
- Various social benefits provided to all affected groups, eg Income Support, Housing Benefit. Welfare Reform Act introducing the Universal Benefit which contains a Personal Independence payment.

Women
- Protection from discrimination through the Equality Act (2010), replacing various pieces of legislation.
- Various social benefits provided to all affected groups, eg Income Support, Housing Benefit. Welfare Reform Act introducing the Universal Benefit which will encourage claimants back into work.

2. *Candidates can be credited in a number of ways **up to a maximum of 6 marks**. Answers which explain why people have good health or others do not have good health or a combination of the two approaches to explaining the issue will be credited.*

Possible approaches to answering the question:

Some people have good health because they eat vegetables.
[1 mark—accurate but undeveloped point]

Some people have good health because they take regular exercise which keeps their heart fit and strong.
[2 marks—accurate point with development]

Some people have poor health as they may live in a poor quality house. If they have inadequate heating or their house is damp then conditions like asthma and bronchitis are more likely.
[3 marks—accurate point with development and exemplification]

Some people have poor health due to the choices they make in the way they live their lives. Smokers are more likely to develop lung cancer, drinkers are more likely to damage their liver and those who abuse heroin are more likely to fall victim to HIV/AIDS. People choose to do these things but they are also linked to poverty, ie people who live in poverty are more likely to choose to abuse themselves in these ways. This is shown by the fact that life expectancy in Scotland's poorest areas is almost twenty years less than in its wealthiest areas.
[4 marks—relevant, accurate point with development, analysis and exemplification]

- Lifestyle factors—eg the effects of smoking, drink/alcohol abuse, lack of exercise.
- Social and economic disadvantages—eg poor diet, effects of poverty.
- Geography and environment—eg poor quality housing, limited access to local amenities, high levels of crime.

- Age—The older you are the more likely you are to suffer poor health.
- Gender—Women live longer than men but are more likely to suffer poor health.
- Race—High incidence of heart attacks, strokes, depression etc amongst some ethnic minorities. Also more likely to suffer socio-economic disadvantage and therefore suffer ill health due to this.

3. *Candidates can be credited in a number of ways **up to a maximum of 8 marks.***

Possible approaches to answering the question:

Option 1: Danny Wilson is not selective in his view "The homeless problem in Scotland is caused by a lack of available houses."

Candidate should give information that Danny Wilson has selected because it supports his view.

Danny's view is not selective as Source 1 shows that the number of new houses is down 38%.

> [1 mark—accurate use of Source 1 but minimal development]

Danny's view is not selective as Source 1 shows that the number of new houses built in 2011/12 fell to a four-year-low of 15,900 which is not nearly enough to tackle the huge numbers who have been accepted as homeless—35,515 households according to Source 1.

> [2 marks—accurate and detailed use of statistics]

Reference to aspects of the following will be credited:

- The "Right to Buy" policy has reduced the numbers of available homes by 80,411 [S2] which means fewer "decent homes for rental" [S1].
- Only 7,847 council houses are empty [S1] which is not enough considering that over 35,000 households have been accepted as homeless by our local councils. [S1]
- Councils are not building enough new houses, only 5,861 according to Source 2. This is partly due to the 45% cut in the Scottish Government's housing budget [S1] which should be reversed [S3] if the problems are to be tackled.

Option 2: Danny Wilson is selective in his view "The homeless problem in Scotland is caused by a lack of available houses."

Candidate should give information that Danny Wilson has not selected because it does not support his view.

Danny Wilson's view is selective when he says 'the homeless problem in Scotland is caused by a lack of available houses' as source 3 shows that people are made homeless for a variety of reasons which have nothing to do with a shortage of available homes. These include release from prison or hospital, which accounts for 5% of the homeless. Although this is only one in twenty people, the situation has been made worse by massive Government cuts of 45% which has exaggerated the problem for vulnerable groups [S3] and not helped the charities like SACRO and APEX who have limited funding. [S1 and S3]

> [3 marks—accurate information from two sources with some evaluative terminology used regarding the statistic included, ie "only one in twenty" and "massive"]

Reference to aspects of the following will be credited:

- Over 40% of homeless people are homeless because of reasons including being intimidated by anti-social (S1) or violent neighbours (S3). This accounts for 5% of the homeless and is not caused by a lack of housing.
- Some people become homeless because they do not pay their rent or mortgage. This is a small figure (5%) but it is not caused by a lack of housing as there are 87,000 empty houses in Scotland and 7,847 empty council houses.
- Danny is selective because a comparison of all types of empty houses (S1) (87,000) and the numbers who are homeless (35,515) show that there are more than enough available houses to meet demand.
- Homelessness has fallen by 2,585 households since 2010–11, accompanied by a fall in new houses. If a shortage of houses was to blame then homelessness would have gone up.

Part D

1. *Candidates can be credited in a number of ways **up to a maximum of 6 marks.***

Possible approaches to answering the question:

The police try to reduce crime by arresting suspects.

> [1 mark—accurate but undeveloped point]

The police try to reduce crime levels by promoting crime prevention campaigns such as "Neighbourhood Watch".

> [2 marks—accurate point with development]

The police try to reduce crime levels by working in the community. They visit schools to talk to pupils and some schools have "campus" officers who try to get to know pupils and steer them clear of trouble. In my school many pupils attend regular "Blue Light" discos organised by the local police officers.

> [3 marks—accurate point with development and exemplification]

- Maintain law and order by having foot patrol officers "on the beat".
- Detect crimes, eg carry out investigations, interview witnesses, process evidence. Role of CID.
- Crime prevention, eg visiting schools, Neighbourhood Watch.
- Highly visible presence at public events, eg security at football matches.
- Initiatives, eg knife amnesties.
- Work with community groups and charities such as APEX.

2. *Candidates can be credited in a number of ways **up to a maximum of 6 marks.***

Possible approaches to answering the question:

Some people commit crime because they are bored.

> [1 mark—accurate but undeveloped point]

Some people commit crime because they are addicted to drugs and steal things to pay for these.

> [2 marks—accurate point with development]

Some people commit crime because they are influenced by those around them. Peer pressure is very important especially amongst young people who feel excluded from society. Some young people can be encouraged into drug taking and crime just for the "thrill".

> [3 marks—accurate point with development and exemplification]

People commit crime for numerous reasons. Many offenders come from deprived areas and feel a sense of hopelessness about their future. However, "white collar crime" seems to be motivated by greed. Many very rich people in the financial industries have been guilty of theft and fraud despite the fact that they appear to have everything they need. Many see "white collar crime" as inevitable as people are bound to be tempted by the huge sums of money that they manage. A recent example of "white collar crime" was the scandal over MPs' expenses.

[4 marks—relevant, accurate point with development, analysis and exemplification]

- Family background, criminal behaviour within family.
- Peer pressure/role models.
- Alienation from society.
- Poor environment.
- Social and economic circumstances.
- Criminal behaviour while young.
- Thrill seeking.
- Response to poverty/economic inequality.
- Greed.
- Opportunistic crime.
- Link with alcohol/drug use
- Impact of violent media.

3. *Candidates can be credited in a number of ways* **up to a maximum of 8 marks.**

Possible approaches to answering the question:

Option 1: Billy Mackenzie is not selective in his view, "Giving anyone caught carrying a knife a prison sentence is a good way to reduce knife crime."

Candidate should give information that Billy Mackenzie has selected because it supports his view.

Billy's view is not selective as Source 2 supports his view because the number of convictions for carrying a knife is higher in 2007/08 compared with 1998/99.

[1 mark—accurate use of source 2 but minimal development]

Billy's view is not selective as Source 2 supports his view because the number of convictions for carrying a knife has risen in most years from 1998/99 when it was about 7,000 until it reached a peak in 2006/07 at over 10,000.

[2 marks—accurate and detailed use of statistics]

Reference to aspects of the following will be credited:

- Community groups have called on the Government to take action on deterring young people from carrying such weapons (Source 1) backed by "People are worried about crime." (Source 3).
- The number of people sent to prison for carrying a knife in public fell to a five-year-low in 2008 when only one in three offenders were jailed (Source 1) backed by rise in number of murders with knives at its peak (53%) (Source 2) showing current system not working.
- 1,200 offenders were sentenced for possession of a knife or offensive weapon between 2004 and 2009, but only 314 were given custodial terms (Source 1) backed by percentage of murders with knives rising from 37% in 2005 to 48% in 2007 and handling an offensive weapon rising from around 9,000 to 10,000 in Source 2.
- In 2009, one in five people convicted of carrying a knife or offensive weapon in Edinburgh had previously been charged for a similar offence (Source 1) shows current sentences do not deter the carrying of knives. This is backed by 78% of Glasgow youths who said they would stop carrying a knife if they were given a prison sentence (Source 1).

Option 2: Billy Mackenzie is selective in his view, "Giving anyone caught carrying a knife a prison sentence is a good way to reduce knife crime."

Candidate should give information that Billy Mackenzie has not selected because it does not support his view.

Billy Mackenzie's view is being selective when it says 'giving all people caught carrying a knife a prison sentence is a good way to reduce knife crime' as only 30% of young people thought that introducing tougher sentences would reduce knife crime which is quite a small percentage and this is supported by Louise McKay who says that locking up people who carry knives is not the answer to tackling this problem.

[3 marks—accurate information from two sources with some evaluative terminology used regarding the statistic included, ie 'only' and 'quite a small percentage']

Reference to aspects of the following will be credited:

- Scottish Prisons reported that as a result of overcrowding, offenders were not serving their full sentence and were being released early (Source 1). This shows that introducing mandatory sentencing will only crowd prisons further.
- 30% of young people thought that introducing tougher sentences would reduce knife crime (Source 1) which is a minority backed by Source 3. "Locking up people is not the answer..."
- 53% of teens questioned thought that community sentences were an appropriate punishment for young people found carrying a knife. Backed by Source 3. "Community projects would help young people realise how much damage they can do themselves and others by carrying a knife. ..." (Source 3).

Section 3

Part E

1. *Candidates can be credited in a number of ways* **up to a maximum of 4 marks.**

Possible approaches to answering the question:

Citizens can participate in politics by joining a political party.

[1 mark—accurate but undeveloped point]

People in Australia can participate in politics by voting in elections when they are 18 or over.

[2 marks—accurate point with development]

American citizens can participate in politics by joining an interest group that they agree with (eg the National Rifle Association) and helping to campaign for certain laws. The NRA supports the right to own guns in the USA and citizens could take part in legal activities such as marches, rallies, petitions, letter writing to Senators etc.

[3 marks—accurate point with development and exemplification]

Reference to aspects of the following will be credited:

- voting in elections at various levels
- membership of political parties
- standing as a candidate in elections
- fundraising
- party activism
- interest group membership and activity
- protest/direct action

2. *Candidates can be credited in a number of ways* **up to a maximum of 6 marks.** *Answers which explain social inequalities, economic inequalities or a combination of the two will be credited.*

Possible approaches to answering the question:

Inequality exists in the USA as some people do badly at school.

[1 mark—accurate but undeveloped point]

In China, some people in rural areas still rely on traditional methods of healthcare, unlike the modern methods and equipment in the towns.

[2 marks—accurate point with development]

In Canada, some people are very wealthy while others have low incomes. Canada is a capitalist country and so people who succeed in business can become very wealthy. Other groups who may have poor qualifications may be stuck in low paid jobs or be reliant on benefits.

[3 marks—accurate point with development and exemplification]

Many people in India live in very poor housing conditions. Indian cities have grown rapidly in recent years as India is one of the fastest growing economies in the world. Many people live in poorly constructed shanty towns or slums which are unsafe and unhealthy. Although some Indians are very rich, most are poor and work in unskilled jobs and so can only afford to live in these poor areas. People who live in these slums are more likely to suffer ill-health, be the victims of crime and experience lack of success in education. This means that housing inequalities will continue.

[4 marks—relevant, accurate point with development, analysis and exemplification]

Reference to aspects of the following will be credited:

- education inequalities
- health inequalities
- employment/unemployment
- wealth/poverty
- housing
- gender inequalities
- racial inequalities
- social class inequalities

3. *Candidates can be credited in a number of ways up to a maximum of 10 marks.*

Possible approaches to answering the question:

Option 1: Build the Melo Bonte Dam

The Government should build the Melo Bonte Dam as it is vital for the continued expansion of the economy, as the growing population needs more electricity.

[1 mark—evidence drawn from Source 1]

The Government should build the Melo Bonte Dam as it is vital for the continued expansion of the economy, as Source 1 says that most people support the decision to build the dam and this is backed up by the opinion poll in Source 2 which shows 65% of all people agree with the decision to build the dam.

[2 marks—evidence linked from Source 1 and Source 2]

Reference to aspects of the following will be credited:

- The Minister of Mines and Energy said the Melo Bonte complex, to be built near the mouth of the Celdy River in the rainforest, will "play an important role in the development" of the area and people displaced by the dam "will be compensated." (Source 1).
- The Government says the dam is vital for the continued expansion of the economy as the country needs more electricity (Source 1).
- The dam has been defended by some in the local population who hope to benefit from the estimated 18,000 direct jobs and 80,000 indirect jobs the Government says the project would create. (Source 1)
- The Melo Bonte Dam is expected to provide electricity to 23 million homes.
- The Government said that most people support the decision to build the dam (Source 1).

- 65% of the population agreed with the Government's decision to build the Melo Bonte Dam (Source 2).
- June 20, Many indigenous people back the dam because it will generate employment to replace the jobs lost since a clamp down on illegal logging (Source 3).
- July 15, The companies building the dam agree to pay US$803 million to create parks and help monitor forests and to pay compensation to people affected by the dam (Source 3).

Reasons for rejecting other option:

I rejected the option to not build the dam as, although protesters say the dam could cause serious damage to the rainforest and the lives of up to 50,000 rainforest residents could be affected, Source 3 says the companies building the dam agree to pay US$803 million to create parks and help monitor forests and to pay compensation to people affected by the dam. [2 marks]

Option 2: Do not build the Melo Bonte Dam

The Government should not build the Melo Bonte Dam as protesters say the proposed dam would cause serious damage to the rainforest and the lives of up to 50,000 rainforest residents could be affected (Source 1). In an opinion poll only 12% of rainforest residents agreed and a large majority of 85% said they disagreed with the decision to build the dam.

[3 marks—evidence linked from Source 1 (1 mark) with detailed use of evidence from Source 2 demonstrating evaluative terminology (2 marks)].

Reference to aspects of the following will be credited:

Arguments to oppose the building of the Melo Bonte Dam

- The project has raised a storm of protest, with judges, Hollywood celebrities, environmental pressure groups and local people in opposition (Source 1).
- In April 2010, *Avatar* director James Cameron and two members of the film's cast, took part in protests (Source 1).
- Protesters say the proposed dam would cause "serious damage" to the rainforest ecosystem, and the lives of up to 50,000 people could be affected as 500 square kilometres could be flooded (Source 1).
- Some experts and business representatives in the energy industry also oppose the dam. They say the actual cost will be 60% higher than its US$10.8 billion budget and will only operate at 40% of its installed capacity, due to the drop in water in the Celdy River during the dry season (Source 1).
- In an opinion poll 85% of rainforest residents disagreed with the Government's decision to build the Melo Bonte Dam (Source 2).
- Over half of people think that environmental damage is the main priority facing the country (Source 2).
- 62% of people think the health service is the main priority facing the country (Source 2).
- April 12, international celebrities attend protests with over 500 protesters to demand the cancellation of the project to build the Melo Bonte Dam (Source 3).
- April 15, under pressure from local people and campaigners, local politicians obtain a court injunction to ban companies bidding to build the dam (Source 3).
- July 2, Campaigners say they will continue protesting despite the contract being awarded (Source 3).

Reasons for rejecting other option:

I rejected the option to build the dam as there have been a storm of protests from Hollywood celebrities and environmental pressure groups and organisations representing rainforest residents. [1 mark awarded for use of one piece of information from Source 1 with no linking. Do not credit if marks already awarded for this point.]

Part F

1. *Candidates can be credited in a number of ways **up to a maximum of 4 marks**.*

Possible approaches to answering the question:

The World Bank gives loans to countries.
[1 mark—accurate but undeveloped point]

The African Union try to help stop conflicts between countries in Africa by holding peace talks with their leaders.
[2 marks—accurate point with development]

The United Nations has tried to help refugees in many poor areas in the world. Recently, they have been providing emergency medicines, shelters and clean water to people in the "Horn of Africa" as they suffered a very serious drought. Many people walked hundreds of miles to refugee camps just to get basic food and clean water.
[3 marks—accurate point with development and exemplification]

Reference to aspects of the following will be credited:

United Nations Organisation
The United Nations responds to international problems largely through its "Specialised Agencies".

UNICEF
- Agency involved in helping meet the specific needs of children.
- Oral Rehydration Therapy across Africa.
- Campaign in southern Africa to prevent AIDS transmission from mothers to children—setting up clinics, school visits and poster/TV campaigns.
- Campaign to help child soldiers in Sudan—'de-mob' camps.

WHO
- Agency involved in helping meet African health needs.
- Research into Africa's killer diseases such as AIDS and malaria.
- Building and equipping of clinics across Africa such as recently in Congo.
- Campaign to increase the number of blood donors in Ethiopia. This also includes training and education programmes.
- Ongoing vaccination programmes against polio across Sub-Saharan Africa.
- Donation of ICT equipment to African health ministries to help coordinate healthcare and use of health resources.
- Supporting charity campaigns to donate old spectacles to Africa.

UNESCO
- Agency involved in helping meet African education, cultural and science needs.
- Setting up world heritage sites to protect African heritage.
- Teacher Training in Sub-Saharan Africa (TTISSA) campaign.
- The LIFE campaign—Literacy Initiative for Empowerment.
- The School in a Suitcase campaign. All the equipment to run a classroom anywhere, in one bag.
- EDUCAIDS—campaign to improve AIDS education across Africa.
- Education for all by 2015. UNESCO's major campaign to try to meet the Millennium Development goals.

FAO
- Agency mainly concerned with the production of food in Africa and in helping develop agricultural efficiency.
- Recent campaign against high food prices.
- Help for small farmers to increase production, eg emergency rice programme in west Africa.
- Campaigns to protect vulnerable crops against virus and disease, eg cassava.
- Campaigns to educate farmers on the use of fertilizers and farm machinery.
- Funding of research into GM seeds and other "bio-agriculture".

WFP
- Prepare reports which help National Governments and NGOs understand more clearly what the problems are with food security, nutrition, health and education within a country.
- Reduce hunger and under-nutrition everywhere.
- Save lives and protect livelihoods in emergencies by getting food to where it is most needed and quickly. The WFP does this by launching appeals to the international community for funds and food aid.
- The WFP relies entirely on voluntary contributions to finance its operations.
- Restore and rebuild lives after emergencies.

The Security Council
The UN Security Council is a small body of fifteen member states (Five permanent members and 10 non-permanent members, elected for a two-year term). Ambassadors from the fifteen countries can meet at short notice in response to global security issues. They discuss these matters and can pass resolutions which can include military intervention, sanctions, peace keeping missions, mediation etc.

NATO
- NATO has tried to respond to terrorism (9/11 attacks, London underground bombings, Madrid bombings, Glasgow airport attack) by launching operations in Afghanistan and Iraq as part of the "War on Terror". Also involvement in Libya.
- NATO's Defence Against Terrorism Programme established in 2004. NATO has responded to attempts by countries such as Iran to build nuclear weapons by introducing sanctions on trade etc, with the cooperation of the UN Security Council. There have also been diplomatic discussions to further reduce and possibly eliminate entire classes of nuclear weapons.
- NATO has an international naval force patrolling piracy "hotspots" especially off the coast of north-east Africa.
- Developing new missile defence systems to protect NATO countries.
- Cyber security—A major cyber-attack on Estonia, a NATO member, in 2007 by Russian hackers. China "hijacking" 15 per cent of the world's Internet traffic in 2010. More training in cyber defence for NATO members. Better early warning systems to protect NATO members from cyber-attack.

World Bank
- The World Bank is an international financial institution that provides loans to developing countries for capital programs.
- The World Bank funds projects aimed at tackling poverty, increase foreign investment in poor countries, increase international trade etc.
- Haiti was helped to rebuild housing and infrastructure, ICT training has been provided in many African countries, banks in countries such as Nepal have been supported through the worldwide recession.

- Loans have been provided across the world to support education, medicine and clean water projects.

European Union
- Co-operation between member states, eg Irish financial crisis or Greek financial bailout. Attempts to create international economic stability.
- Regional aid bringing investment and jobs, eg infrastructure into places likes the Highlands and Islands helping inequalities across the Union. Freedom of movement also helps to solve inequality. Regional aid benefits Europe's poorer nations.
- Attempts through the CFP and CAP to safeguard food supplies and to conserve fish stocks.
- The EU tries to promote peace and security and has become involved in areas outside Europe in recent year. In 2004, Eufor took over peace keeping in Bosnia-Herzegovina providing over 6,000 troops. The European Defence Force (EDF) has also been involved in the Democratic Republic of Congo, Georgia, Indonesia, Sudan and Palestine. Most recently the EU was involved in Libya.
- Humanitarian aid is given (eg Libya) in partnership with the UN and other NGOs. It assists refugees, treats the injured, prevents human rights abuses and meets other basic needs.
- The EU tries to create jobs and prosperity across its member states through the European Single Currency.

African Union
- Organisation of African countries which aims to promote and improve peace and security, improve the socio/economic lives of Africans and promote democracy and human rights.
- The AU has been central to the fight against AIDS. They have supported education programmes as well as funding treatment centres and training specialist staff.
- The AU tried to help negotiate a peaceful settlement to the Libyan civil war in 2011. The AU has been involved in "conflict resolution" during several African wars.
- AU troops have been active as peacekeepers and as combatants in Somalia, fighting against al-Shabab.
- The AU has captured, detained and tried suspected war criminals from various African conflicts.

Charities and other NGOs
- Expect reference to charities such as Oxfam, Save the Children, The Red Cross etc.
- Medical aid, nurses, doctors, medicines.
- Food aid, provided during times of crisis such as drought or civil war.
- Emergency relief during refugee crisis, eg food, clean water, vaccinations, shelter, other medical treatments.

2. *Candidates can be credited in a number of ways up to a maximum of 6 marks.*

Possible approaches to answering the question:

Poverty has caused a lot of illegal immigration.
[1 mark—accurate but undeveloped point]

Many people have been forced to leave their homes and become refugees in Africa, due to a serious famine and civil war.
[2 marks—accurate point with development]

Many ships have been hijacked by pirates in the Indian Ocean. Many of these pirates have come from Somalia where there is no real government and people are desperately poor. Tourist yachts are seen as an easy target and several British tourists have been kidnapped and held for ransom.

[3 marks—accurate point with development and exemplification]

Terrorism is a major problem, caused by feelings of injustice among some groups. In the last ten years some extremists have become so angry at the USA's domination of the world that they have targeted their buildings and citizens. Several US officials were recently killed in Libya. Al Qaeda is an organisation that has vowed to attack the USA and its allies (such as the UK) as they claim they are "anti-Muslim". Other terrorist organisations exist, including extremists in Northern Ireland who still oppose British government in Ulster.
[4 marks—relevant, accurate point with development, analysis and exemplification]

Reference to aspects of the following will be credited:

Poverty
- war
- unfair trade
- poor education
- poor health
- lack of foreign investment
- few natural economic resources

War
- land disputes
- religious disputes
- ideological disputes
- historical disputes
- expansion ambitions of governments

Piracy
- poverty
- break down of law and order in certain parts of Africa

Disease (HIV /AIDS is likely but not the only acceptable context)
- poor health education
- traditional communities suspicious of modern medical practices
- little availability of drugs/treatments/trained staff
- poor diet
- poor housing
- poor sanitation

3. *Candidates can be credited in a number of ways up to a maximum of 10 marks.*

Possible approaches to answering the question:

For option 1: Country A
Country A should be allowed to join the EU as many drug dealers have been sent to prison.
[1 mark—one piece of evidence from one source]

I rejected the second option (allowing country B to join) as over one third (36%) of its population still work in agriculture. This is nine times the level in the EU (4%) which would not allow the EU to reduce its huge expenditure on agriculture which stands at almost half of the entire budget (48%). Many of the EU members see a drop in this 48% as essential.
[3 marks—accurate information from two sources with some evaluative comment]

- Country A's police have done well in clamping down on drug trafficking. According to the EU opinion survey, 88% of Europeans saw this as fairly important or very important.
- 88% of respondents in the survey also saw a good human rights record as fairly or very important. Country A would meet the criteria for the ECHR.

- University entrants in Country A have been growing in number and are getting close to the EU average of 51%. The EU's economy needs more university graduates.

Against option 1: Country A

Several member states have become concerned about the number of poor countries who are applying to join the EU. Country A's average income (11,200) is less than half of the EU average (23,100).

- The EU takes good care of vulnerable groups, like children. Country A would struggle to meet these standards as shown in a recent UNICEF investigation, which criticized it for "terrible conditions".

For option 2: Country B

Country B should be allowed to join the EU as it produces 32 million barrels of oil and the EU doesn't want to rely on Russia.

[2 marks—evidence linked from Source 1 and Source 2]

I rejected country A as its average income is €11,200. In the EU it is €23,100.

[2 marks awarded for use of two pieces of evidence from different sources. Do not credit if marks already awarded for this point in justification of choice.]

- Country B is self-sufficient in oil and is already producing 19 million barrels per day more than it uses. EU dependence on Russia would be reduced. This would be good as many would like to admit countries with oil reserves.
- 100% in the survey said that low unemployment was fairly important or very important. The graph shows that Country B's unemployment rate is consistently less than the EU average.
- Country B has been praised for reducing illiteracy rates to below 10%. This is coming close to the levels achieved by schools in the EU.

Against option 2: Country B

- Country B has a huge agricultural industry. Over one third of workers are employed in this sector. This would make it difficult to reduce the EU's agriculture budget, which the member states see as necessary.
- Country B has poor health care. Life expectancy is twenty years below the EU average and infant mortality rate is more than double.

NATIONAL 5 MODERN STUDIES MODEL PAPER 1

Section 1

Part A

1. Credit reference to aspects of the following:
   - Make decisions about Education so affects availability of schools etc.
   - Social housing affects the standards of housing in an area
   - Cleansing and recycling means refuse is taken away so areas are cleaner
   - Social work helps peoples' lives by supporting vulnerable groups
   - Community care affects the lives of elderly etc.
   - Decisions about Council Tax affect how much people have to pay

   Below is a model paragraph answer — 3 marks awarded.

   Local Councils affect the lives of Scottish people in many ways. One way is through the collection of refuse or waste. In some local authorities there are many different collections. This may be to try and increase recycling or 'greener' ways of reusing our waste. An example would be North Lanarkshire who have collections for Garden waste, collections for paper and other recyclables, 'food only' waste bins as well as general waste. **4**

2. Credit reference to aspects of the following:

   Happy with the way AMS has worked:
   - Fairer/more proportional so voters' choices more likely to be reflected in Parliament
   - Each voter has two votes so able to split vote — greater choice
   - More representatives to choose from ie constituency and 7 regional MSPs
   - Has resulted in 8 years of coalition government with reasonable stability as well as produced one minority and one majority government — with a reasonable degree of success (so far)

   Unhappy with the way AMS has worked:
   - Complex voting system may cause confusion as in 2007 with many 'lost' or 'wasted' votes
   - Two types of MSP elected with some confusion over roles
   - Not completely proportional — still over-represents larger parties ie Labour and SNP while under-representing smaller parties

   Below is a model paragraph answer — 4 marks awarded.

   One way people are happy with the Additional Member System is the greater representation of smaller parties. In AMS, voters have two votes, one for an individual constituency MSP like Fiona McLeod with the 2nd vote being for a party. From this Regional List MSPs such as Annabel Goldie are created using the d'Hont formula which gives smaller parties greater representation. For example, in every election since 1999 the Green Party has had representation in the parliament.

   8

3. You are required to evaluate a limited range of sources detecting and explaining instances of exaggeration and/or selective use of facts, giving developed answers.

To achieve full marks you must show evidence that has been selected as it supports the view and show evidence that has not been selected, as it does not support the view.

An answer which deals with only one side of your explanation will be awarded a maximum of 6 marks.

Below is a model answer — awarded full marks 8/8.

Gillian Duffy is not being selective when she says "new tax raising powers for the Scottish Parliament would be good for Scotland" as Source 1 states that this would make the Scottish Parliament more accountable as voters could choose the party which had the tax and spending policies they supported. Again Source 1 states that this proposal is the next step to increase the powers of the devolved Parliament now that it has been established for over 20 years. These views are supported in Source 3 which shows that the Scottish public overwhelmingly trust the Scottish Government more than the UK Government — 60% to only 24 % — so it would be good for Scotland.

Gillian Duffy is being selective as Source 1 states that this change could lead to higher taxes in Scotland compared to England, which could be bad and it could reduce the influence of the UK Government. In source 2 we see that the public think that the UK Government has the most influence over the way Scotland is run and this is the way it should be as in Source 1 the Scottish Government only has devolved powers.

She is also being selective as Source 1 states that new tax powers would give the UK Government an excuse to reduce the funding to the Scottish Government and Parliament and this could lead to less spending on health and education and this could make the Scottish Government less popular and reduce trust. This could be problem as in Source 3 we see that trust in the Scottish Parliament has declined from 70% in 2007 to 60% in 2009.   **8**

Part B

1. Credit reference to aspects of the following:
   - Discusses laws in depth as they have time
   - Brings experience to discussions
   - Can delay legislation
   - May be able to force government to rethink legislation or policy
   - Can be used to 'elevate' former senior MPs etc.
   - Can bring ministers into the Government

Below is a model paragraph answer — 3 marks awarded.

One way in which the Lords can play a part in decision making is that it can amend most bills if the majority of peers have issues with some of the details. For example, the coalition government's Health and Social Care Bill experienced a number of amendments as it passed through the Lords including setting up patient councils in England & Wales to monitor healthcare.   **4**

2. Credit reference to aspects of the following:

Positive:
   - Media — Provide information for voters about political issues so makes them more informed as voters
   - Media — Exposes wrongdoing on the part of politicians and parties and so holds them to account
   - Media — Broadcast media such as TV and Radio need to be neutral and objective
   - Trade Unions — Provide an influential body to promote workers' rights and conditions

   - Trade Unions — their peaceful protests help promote democracy
   - Trade Unions — their relationship with the Labour party provides representation for all sections of society
   - Pressure Groups — help provide influence for minority groups
   - Pressure Groups — provide information for voters about political issues
   - Pressure Groups — keep people involved in politics due to popularity

Negative:
   - Media — Newspapers concentrate on scandal and create a cynical attitude amongst voters leading to decline in interest in politics and voting
   - Media--Some newspapers are not serious and trivialise and over simplify matters which leaves voters less well informed
   - Media — Some newspapers are very biased and do not give voters a balanced view of issues
   - Trade Unions — they can hold the Government to ransom through the threat of strike
   - Trade Unions — some feel their relationship with the Labour party has too much influence on decision-making
   - Trade Unions — can cause disruption for many people — BA strikes
   - Pressure Groups — sometimes give a minority too much influence
   - Pressure Groups — Occasionally protests can turn violent/disruptive — eg 2011 student riots
   - Pressure Groups — some PGs are very large and through lobbying can have too much influence over government policy

Below is a model paragraph answer — 4 marks awarded.

Some people think that the media plays a positive role in politics as it gives political parties an opportunity to inform voters about party policies. During election time, there are party political broadcasts on the TV. The time that is given to these broadcasts are based on the balance of power in parliament, therefore, they are fair. These party political broadcasts are usually on TV at peak times thus reaching as wide an audience as possible. Watching these broadcasts allow voters to use their vote in an informed way.   **8**

3. You are required to evaluate a limited range of sources, detecting and explaining instances of exaggeration and/or selective use of facts, giving developed arguments.

To achieve full marks you must show evidence that has been selected as it supports the view and show evidence that has not been selected, as it does not support the view.

An answer that deals with only one side of the explanation, will only be awarded a maximum of 6 marks.

Below is a model answer — awarded full marks 8/8.

Adam Stewart is being selective when he says "The party leaders' debates in the 2010 election had little impact on the election campaign" as according to Source 1, millions of viewers watched the debates and turnout increased by 4% compared with 2005. This is further supported by Source 3 which shows viewing figures of 9.4m, 4.1m and 8.4m for the three leaders' debates.

Adam Stewart is also being selective as according to Source 1 it was the first time in the UK televised leaders' debates were held and in source 2 it states that a massive 69% of people felt it was a positive change in the election.

However, Adam Stewart is not being selective when he says "The party leaders' debates in the 2010 election had little impact on the election campaign" as according to Source 1 Conservatives were predicted to win and they were the largest party after the election. Also he is not being selective as according to Source 2 some people believed the debates would have little impact on the result as most people have made up their minds, before the election, about who they will vote for. In fact, according to Source 2, a huge 68% felt that the debates would make no difference. **8**

Section 2

Part C

1. Credit reference to aspects of the following:

Scottish Government:
- Smoking ban
- Other actions to reduce smoking e.g. age of purchase, display of cigarettes
- Measures to reduce alcohol consumption — minimum pricing
- Role of NHS Scotland in improving health — advertising, eg 5-a-day
- NHS Health Scotland
- Health Promoting Schools

Local Councils:
- Free access to leisure facilities for school children
- Healthy eating initiatives in schools
- Free school meals P1-3

Below is a model paragraph answer — 3 marks awarded.

The Scottish Government has introduced a number of laws to improve health such as the smoking ban. The smoking ban was introduced in 2006 and banned smoking in public places such as bars and restaurants. This has reduced the amount of people smoking and the amount of people affected by passive smoking — due to this, cancer rates have fallen. **4**

2. Credit reference to aspects of the following:
- Low pay leading to low living standards
- Unemployment leading to reliance on benefits
- Lone parents/family structure
- Alcohol/drugs addiction — leading to unemployment
- Lack of skills/qualifications — confined to low-paid, insecure jobs
- Lack of suitable/well-paid employment because of decline of industry in certain areas

Below is a model paragraph answer — 4 marks awarded.

A reason people live in poverty is due to unemployment. The current recession in the UK has led to high levels of unemployment and many people find themselves out of work. Living on benefits does not provide adequate income and a person who has been unemployed for a long period will struggle to make ends meet and suffer from social exclusion. Long-term unemployment is a major concern for the UK Government and a main reason for people finding themselves stuck in the poverty trap. **6**

3. You must use a limited range of sources by selecting evidence from them in order to make and justify a decision/recommendation.

You will be awarded up to three marks for a justification depending on relevance and development of the evidence.

You will be highly credited if you make justifications which show interaction between the sources.

For full marks, you must justify your decision/recommendation and explain why you have rejected the other option. Answers, which deal with only one decision, will be awarded a maximum of eight marks.

Across the whole answer you must use all 3 sources to achieve full marks.

Below is a model answer — awarded full marks 10/10.

In my role as government advisor I have decided to recommend Option 1 that the Government should continue with the system of Working Tax Credits (WTC).

The first reason to back my recommendation is found in Source 1 where it states that "over half a million children have been lifted out of poverty as more people on low or moderate incomes have been helped." This benefit is highlighted in Source 2 where figures show that child poverty figures have declined. In 2001 3 million children lived in poverty and by 2010 this figure was 2.5 million. The Government Spokesperson in Source 3 underlines this reason stating "the tax credit system has helped many families to get out of poverty." If WTCs are reducing poverty they should be continued.

Another reason to back Option 1 is found in Source 1 where it states "Working Tax Credit allows families to get back up to 80% of the cost of child care allowing adults to go back to work." This links in with Source 3 where the Government Spokesperson states that "Working Tax Credits encourage people to work and also gives help with child care costs." In allowing people to get back to work in this way WTCs should undoubtedly continue.

Lastly, Source 3 states "the problem faced by many was that if they came off benefits and went into low paid jobs, they were worse off." Working Tax Credits have stopped this as Source 1 points out "Working Tax Credits have helped people to beat the poverty trap — it makes sure a person's income is better in work than out of work and living on benefits."

The reason I didn't choose option 2 is, although Source 1 states "there have been problems with overpayments being made", the Government Spokesperson in Source 3 states "despite problems in overpayments in the first few years, many of these difficulties have been sorted." **10**

Part D

1. Credit reference to aspects of the following:
- Vandalism
- Shoplifting
- Breach of the peace
- Under-age drinking — related crimes
- Drug offences
- Graffiti
- Car theft
- Hanging around the streets/causing a disturbance

Below is a model paragraph answer — 3 marks awarded.

If young people do commit crimes they tend to be crimes associated with anti-social behaviour. Young people may drink alcohol and then be more likely to cause breach of the peace. This could include hanging about housing estates or shops in gangs and partaking in rowdy behaviour. **4**

2. Credit reference to aspects of the following:

Community Policing :
- In residential areas where the police can get to know the residents and local young people
- People feel safer in their communities knowing there are police on the beat
- Young people may respond to community initiatives and be less likely to vandalise/get involved in anti-social behaviour
- People may not want CCTV cameras in their local communities

CCTV Cameras:
- In shopping centres/High Streets where shoplifting and pick-pocketing is a problem
- In areas where recording the entrances and exits to facilities will help to identify those who have committed crimes
- Too expensive to police such large areas
- A police presence may not be desirable

Below is a model paragraph answer — 4 marks awarded.

> People believe community policing is effective as it allows the police to get to know local residents and young people in a certain area and hopefully build relationships that will reduce crime. However, some people argue CCTV is an effective way of tackling crime. In areas such as city centres, CCTV cameras can monitor large areas where the police may not be able to patrol at all times. This can be particularly useful at busy weekend periods such as pub/club closing times. **6**

3. You must use a limited range of sources by selecting evidence from them in order to make and justify a decision/recommendation.

You will be awarded up to three marks for a justification depending on relevance and development of the evidence.

You will be highly credited if you make justifications which show interaction between the sources.

For full marks, you must justify your decision/recommendation and explain why you have rejected the other option. Answers, which deal with only one decision, will be awarded a maximum of eight marks.

Across the whole answer you must use all 3 sources to achieve full marks.

Below is a model answer — awarded full marks 10/10.

> In my role as government advisor I have decided to recommend Option 1 that the DNA database should contain profiles of the whole population.

> Source 1 highlights the first reason for my recommendation as it states "most people would approve of a new law requiring all adults to give a sample of their DNA to help with prevention and detection of crime." This is backed up in Source 2 where it shows that 66% of people polled in an opinion survey agreed that there should be a new law requiring everyone over 18 to give a sample of DNA.

> Another reason to back my recommendation is in Source 1 where it states "ethnic minorities are more likely, at present, to be on the database than white people." This is backed up in Source 2 where figures show that 37% of blacks and 13% of Asians are on the DNA database compared to only 9% of whites. This links with Source 3 where the Police Spokesperson states that "having everyone on the database means there will be no discrimination against ethnic minorities." The race issue

> regarding the database would be solved if everyone gave their DNA.

> Another reason to back option 1 is found in Source 3 where the Police Spokesperson states "DNA evidence… will help the police convict the right person in the most serious of crimes." This is backed up in Source 1 which states "if the whole population had their DNA profiles on the database, this would help in the investigation and prosecution of crime." In the opinion poll in Source 2 65% of people stated that DNA evidence was more important than any other type of evidence. DNA would ultimately help in convicting guilty people.

> I did not choose option 2 as, although the Civil Rights Spokesperson states "the DNA database should be kept for profiles of convicted criminals only", Source 1 states "money and time would be saved if everyone's DNA profile was taken only once." **10**

Section 3

Part E

1. Clear reference to specific political institutions of chosen G20 country. Credit reference to aspects of the following:
- Different levels of government
- Democratic structures
- Voting in elections at various levels
- Opportunities for political participation
- Specific USA reference to aspects of Executive, Legislature and Judiciary and separation of powers

Below is a model paragraph answer — 3 marks awarded.

> The country I have studied is the USA.

> The American Constitution outlines the powers of the different institutions. The President is also elected every four years and they are in charge of the Executive. The President proposes laws which are implemented by Congress and judged legal by the Supreme Court. **6**

2. Credit references to the following:
- Educational inequality issues in your selected country
- Any issues relating to health and healthcare inequalities within your selected country
- Issues relating to law and order within your selected country
- Differences in housing between different groups in your selected country

Below is a model paragraph answer — 4 marks allocated.

> In the USA health inequalities continue to be a problem. In the USA you have to buy private medical insurance from a company such as BlueCross. This means that many people in poverty do not have any medical insurance and so receive only very basic medical care. It is estimated that up to 40 million Americans do not have adequate medical cover. This has led to huge inequalities in some parts of the USA which at times can be related to race with Blacks and Hispanics being more likely to suffer from poverty and not be covered by private medical insurance. **6**

3. You are required to use the sources provided to draw valid conclusions, with supporting evidence

You should draw conclusions using the headings/bullet points in the question.

An answer which merely repeats the source material without making judgements or conclusions will be awarded zero marks.

For full marks three developed conclusions must be given.

You should link information within and between sources in support of your conclusion.

The conclusion can be placed either at the beginning or at the end after the evidence.

Below is a model answer — awarded full marks 8/8.

> *Ethnic composition in different parts of the country*
>
> The conclusion is by far that Han is the largest ethnic group in the G20 country.
>
> According to Source 1, "the largest ethnic group, by far, is the Han". This is supported by Source 3 which shows that 5 out of the 6 regions are dominated by Han. Only Tibet is not dominated by Han.
>
> *The Link between income and education*
>
> The conclusion is that those on lower income are more likely to be unable to read or write.
>
> According to Source 1 there are big differences in levels of income within different parts of the country, with coastal regions having considerably more wealth. Income differences are important because they will have an effect upon education. This is supported by Source 2 which shows that the three inland areas which are poorest have rates that range from 19.7% to 54.9%, whereas in richer coastal areas the figure ranges from 4.6% to 7.6%.
>
> *Health in urban and rural areas*
>
> The conclusion is that rural areas have worse health than urban areas.
>
> According to Source 1 there are big differences in health and education between rural and urban areas. The source goes on to explain that this is because "rural areas are poorer and so too are health facilities". Source 2 further emphasises this by showing that in the three rural areas life expectancy is substantially lower than in the three urban areas. In fact, in the most rural area Tibet, life expectancy is 64 years old contrasting with the most urban area Shanghai in which life expectancy is 78. **8**

Part F

1. Credit reference to aspects of the following:

   Issue — Terrorism:
   - Nationalism — Palestine/Israel
   - Political unrest — Syria
   - Religious Extremism — Afghanistan/Taliban/Al Qaeda
   - Discrimination
   - Poverty

   Below is a model paragraph answer — 3 marks awarded.

   > There are various causes of terrorism. Firstly, a group may resort to terrorist acts to try to achieve a nationalist goal. This means they believe their region or country should have independence from another country. A group of people may not believe national independence is possible through the ballot box and in turn decide to turn to terrorist methods to achieve their aims. **6**

2. Credit reference to aspects of the following:

   Issue — Terrorism:
   - NATO- Difficulties in Afghanistan and Iraq, residence from Taliban and other extremist organisations
   - European Union — sharing of intelligence, human rights
   - United Nations — Differing views of member countries on what constitutes terrorism (USA/Russia on Syria, views on Palestine/Israel etc). Veto of Security Council in dealing with countries that facilitate terrorist activity

   Below is a model paragraph answer — 4 marks awarded.

   > The European Union (EU) has responded to terrorism by increasing cooperation between member states. However, many EU nations have encountered difficulties in dealing with suspected terrorists from other countries as they have not been able to deport them back to their country of origin. Often this is associated with a person's human rights and EU countries have to be careful not to prevent anyone from receiving their human rights as outlined by the UN. **6**

3. You are required to use the sources provided to draw valid conclusions, with supporting evidence

   You should draw conclusions using the headings/bullet points in the question.

   An answer which merely repeats the source material without making judgements or conclusions will be awarded zero marks.

   For full marks three developed conclusions must be given.

   You should link information within and between sources in support of your conclusions.

   The conclusion can be placed either at the beginning or at the end after the evidence.

   Below is a model answer — awarded full marks 8/8.

   > *The success of the G8 in meeting Promise 1: To improve Health Care*
   >
   > The conclusion is that G8 countries have been very successful in meeting Promise 1.
   >
   > Using Source 1, we see that Promise 1 is to improve health and Source 1 also shows that the % of people in Rwanda with HIV decreased from 7.0 in 1996 to 2.8 in 2009. Source 3 provided further evidence of improved health with infant mortality rates declining and life expectancy rising in all three countries. In Malawi, infant mortality rates have declined from 122 in 1996 to 65 in 2009 and in Ethiopia life expectancy has increased from 49 to 56.
   >
   > *The success of the G8 in meeting Promise 2:*
   >
   > The conclusion is that that the G8 countries have not been successful at all in meeting Promise 2.
   >
   > Using Source 1, we see that Promise 2 is to more than double total ODA given to all less developed countries by 2010 and Source 1 also shows that Canada almost reached Promise 2 with its ODA spend increasing from $2.6 billion in 2004 to $5.1 billion in 2010. In Source 2 the figure for the UK went from $7.9 billion to $13.8 billion. Again, this has not more than doubled. This was the same for the other G8 countries in the table, all failed to more than double their ODA contribution.
   >
   > *The G8 country most committed to meeting the UN aid recommendation.*

The conclusion is that the UK is the G8 country most committed to meeting the UN aid recommendation.

In Source 1 it states that the UN recommendation is 0.7% of a country's GNI be set aside as ODA. Source 2 shows that in 2010 the country giving the highest % of GNI as ODA was the UK at 0.56%. This is below the UN recommendation but it does make the UK the most committed G8 country. Italy was the less committed with its % of GNI remaining the same in 2005 and 2010 at 0.15%. All other countries increased their % of GNI but none reached the figure of 0.7%. **8**

NATIONAL 5 MODERN STUDIES MODEL PAPER 2

Section 1

Part A

1. Credit reference to aspects of the following:
   - Health and social work
   - Education and training
   - Local Government and housing
   - Justice and police
   - Agriculture, forestry and fisheries
   - The environment
   - Tourism, sport and heritage
   - Economic development and internal transport

   Below is a model paragraph answer — 3 marks awarded.

   > One devolved matter in which the Scottish government can make decisions is healthcare. All healthcare decisions are made in Scotland for Scotland with decisions about new hospitals and care for the elderly devolved. An example is the Government's decisions to ban the display of cigarettes in large shops to try and stop people being attracted to smoking. **4**

2. Credit reference to aspects of the following:
   - Grants from Scottish Government (revenue and capital)
   - Council Tax
   - Non-domestic Rates
   - Charges for council provided services, including rent
   - Sales
   - PPP projects or similar

   Below is a model paragraph answer — 4 marks awarded.

   > Local Authorities can raise funds in a number of ways. Their main income is from Council Tax which is charged to every household. This tax is used to pay for huge variety of services. For example, Local Authorities provide state education and money raised from council taxes will help pay for local schools and nurseries. Council Tax varies depending on which area you stay in and the number of rooms within the house. **6**

3. You are required to evaluate a limited range of sources, in order to make and justify a decision/recommendation.

   You must also explain why you have rejected the other option.

   In order to achieve full marks you must say why you did not choose the other option. If your answer deals with only one option it will be awarded a maximum of 8 marks.

   Below is a model answer — awarded full marks 10/10.

   > *For Ian McKay*
   >
   > The candidate I would choose would be Ian MacKay. One reason why I chose him is that Ian supports the golf development because he says that a lot of jobs will be provided for the local area. This is true as Source 2 clearly states that the Inverdon Dunes Golf Development will create 5,000 temporary and 1,250 permanent jobs. This will be particularly good for Inverdon as Source 1 shows that unemployment in Inverdon is running at 4.2% which is above the Scottish average of 4%. The possibility of new jobs would, therefore, be most welcome.

   Another reason why I have chosen Ian is his concern about the number of migrant workers moving to the area, and most local people agree. This is supported by the Public

Opinion Survey in Source 3 which shows that 55% think that Inverdon does not need more migrant workers. According to the Source 2 the jobs that will be created will be skilled or highly skilled and according to Source 1 these will not be attractive to migrant workers.

Lastly, Ian also says that, although some wildlife tourists will be lost, many more golf tourists will be attracted. This is supported by Source 2 with the information that 25,000 wildlife tourists visit the area at the moment. However, as many as 100,000 golf tourists could be attracted by the new development.

One reason I did not chose Sally Anderson is that she states that the vast majority of the public agree with her view and do not support the development and don't think the area needs a boost to local businesses. However, Source 3 shows that 65%, which is the majority, say "Yes" to supporting the golf development. This is further backed up by Source 1, which states that the area needs a boost to the local economy. **10**

Part B

1. Credit reference to aspects of the following:

   Help in election campaign by:
   • Canvassing in person
   • Telephone canvassing
   • Delivery of election materials
   • Talking to voters to persuade them to support candidate
   • Administrative work in candidate's office
   • Giving lifts to voters on day of election
   • Taking part in publicity events

   National campaign has major impact on local campaigns:
   • Setting agenda
   • National media campaigns

   Below is a model paragraph answer — 3 marks awarded.

   > Political parties campaign to get their candidates elected by producing a large number and variety of election materials. These take the form of leaflets, placards and posters. Political parties will recruit volunteers to distribute these materials, usually in town or city centres. Quite often political parties will also go door-to-door to try to convince the public to vote for their candidate — this is known as canvassing. **4**

2. Credit reference to aspects of the following:

   Changes:
   • Wish to see all or some of House of Lords elected as it is undemocratic at present
   • Wish to see wider range of members as unrepresentative at moment
   • Wish to see end to patronage as PM/governing party can appoint supporters
   • Wish to see more powers as able to check power of Commons eg power of veto rather than delay only, no power over money bills.
   • Wish to see more modern working practices as many are outdated
   • Wish to see introduction of PR system of voting

   Below is a model paragraph answer — 4 marks awarded.

   > Some people want changes made to the House of Lords as they see it as being undemocratic. At the moment peers are unelected as honours are given out by the Prime Minister for life. Many want there to be elections for some or all peers. They believe that the Lords will then become more accountable and will therefore make decisions with the public interest in mind rather

than another agenda. The Liberal Democrats have long been supporters of reform, however, despite several movements to reform the Upper Chamber, it has remained largely unchanged since the last reforms in 1999. **6**

3. You are required to evaluate a limited range of sources, in order to make and justify a decision/recommendation.

   You must also explain why you have rejected the other option.

   In order to achieve full marks you must say why you did not choose the other option. If your answer deals with only one option it will be awarded a maximum of 8 marks.

   Below is a mode answer — awarded full marks 10/10.

   For Kirsty Reid

   The candidate I would chose is Kirsty Reid as she supports the quarry because it will provide jobs to stop the decline of the local economy. This is backed up by the background information which shows that 150 new jobs will be created in the quarry. This is supported by Source 2 which shows that jobs are the issue that is seen as very important — 52%.

   Also, according to Source 1 there are a number of transport problems in the constituency, including high petrol prices and poor public transport. In Source 3 Kirsty Reid says that she will make improving transport links a priority to attract more business to the area. This will help with a number of issues in Gleninch such as the huge unemployment rate which is 13% above the Scottish average.

   She also states that these jobs are needed to keep young people in the area. This is backed up by Source 1 which states that many young people in the area move away to big cities.

   The reason I did not chose Robbie McKay is because he opposes the new quarry because according to him the local party are more concerned about the environment than jobs. However, this is not true. The survey shows that 52% think that jobs are very important, compared to only 30% for the environment. Also according to Source 1 tourism is becoming less important to the local economy, with those employed in hotels, bed and breakfast accommodation and restaurants on the decline. **10**

Section 2

Part C

1. Credit reference to aspects of the following:
   • Child Benefit – helps families with children under the age of 16
   • Housing Benefit – helps those on a low income to pay their rent
   • Jobseekers Allowance – helps those who are looking for a job
   • State Pension – helps those who have retired
   • Tax Credits – supports families on a low income
   • Educational Maintenance Allowance (EMA)
   • Cold Weather Payments
   • Employment and Support Allowance
   • Income Support
   • Incapacity Benefits

   Below is a model paragraph answer — 3 marks awarded.

   > The Government provides a 'safety net' for the population should a person fall on hard times and

require support – this is called the Welfare State. One way the Government helps people is through various forms of financial support. Firstly, if a person loses their job the Government will help them until they find another. This unemployed benefit is called Job Seekers Allowance, which usually amounts to around £57 per week.   **6**

2. Credit reference to aspects of the following:
   - Lifestyle Factors – eg the effects of smoking, drink/alcohol abuse, lack of exercise
   - Social and Economic disadvantages – eg poor diet, effects of poverty
   - Geography and environment – eg poor quality housing, limited access to local amenities, high levels of crime
   - Gender – Women live longer than men but are more likely to suffer poor health
   - Race – High incidence of heart attacks, strokes, depression etc. Also more likely to be poor and therefore to suffer ill health due to this

   Below is a model paragraph answer – 4 marks awarded.

   > Health inequalities continue to exist in the UK because many people continue to make poor lifestyle choices. Choosing to smoke, excessively drink alcohol and eat a fatty diet can lead to complex health issues such as diabetes, heart attacks and strokes. Life expectancy among people who make poor lifestyle choices and don't exercise is significantly lower than those who choose to lead a healthy life. Across Glasgow there are vast life expectancy differences with poorer people tending to make worse lifestyle choices than those better off.   **6**

3. You are required to use the sources provided to draw valid conclusions, with supporting evidence.

   You should draw conclusions using the headings/bullet points in the question.

   An answer which merely repeats the source material without making judgements or conclusions will be awarded zero marks.

   For full marks three developed conclusions must be given.

   You should link information within and between sources in support of your conclusions.

   The conclusion can be placed either at the beginning or at the end after the evidence.

   Below is a model answer – awarded full marks 8/8.

   > *Changes in marriage and divorce in Britain.*
   >
   > The first conclusion is that the rate of marriages has decreased and the rate of divorces has increased.
   >
   > Source 1 shows that the rate of marriages has fallen by around 50% from 1970 to 2005. The source also shows that the rate of divorces has increased from around 75,000 per year in 1970 to 180,000 in 2005. Source 3 also states "from 1970 to 2005 there has been a large drop in marriages in general but not in divorces."
   >
   > *The link between changes in marriages and changes in the "traditional" family.*
   >
   > Another conclusion is that as the percentage of marriages fell, the percentage of the 'traditional' family fell also.
   >
   > Source 2 states that "the 'traditional' family has always been seen as a couple with dependent children". The % of the 'traditional' family has fallen from 52% of households in 1971 to 35% in 2009. Source 1 highlights

that in the same time period, between 1970 and 2005, marriages have decreased by more than 50%.

> *The main difference between ethnic minority families and white families.*
>
> My final conclusion is that Whites have the lowest percentage of married couples and the highest percentage of lone parent families compared to all other ethnic groups.
>
> Source 3 backs this up, stating that Whites only have a married couple's percentage of 62% where as the table shows Indians at a massive 83% and Bangladeshi, Chinese and Pakistani all ahead of Whites. Indians also have the lowest rate of lone parent families at 12% compared to Whites at 25%. This links in with Source 2 where it states "white people in Britain have the lowest percentage of married couples."   **8**

Part D

1. **Credit reference to aspects of the following:**

   District Court/Justice of the Peace Court
   - The longest prison sentence which can be imposed is generally 60 days
   - The maximum fine of up to £2500
   - Minor offences

   Sheriff Court
   - Summary procedure – a sheriff may impose prison sentences of up to 3 months, in some cases up to 12 months. Fines up to £5000. No Jury Present – Less Serious Cases.
   - Solemn procedure – unlimited financial penalties – can refer to the High Court, also has a range of non-custodial options such as community service and probation. Jury Present – Serious Cases

   High Court (of Justiciary)
   - Judge presides
   - Most serious crimes such as rape, assault and murder
   - Jury of 15
   - Custodial and non-custodial sentencing options

   Court of Session
   - Civil cases

   Below is a model paragraph answer – 3 marks awarded.

   > Within the adult court system in Scotland there are various courts that deal with a range of crimes and offences. Firstly, the Justice of the Peace Courts in Scotland (formerly known as District courts) deal with minor offences such as breach of the peace and driving offences. In these courts there is no jury or judge and sentencing powers are limited to a max fine of £2500 and 60 days in prison.   **6**

2. Credit reference to aspects of the following:
   - Overcrowding and other poor conditions against prisoners' human rights and does not encourage rehabilitation
   - Used too frequently – young people into prison system too early
   - Lack of staff and funding to run rehabilitation programmes
   - High level of recidivism
   - Contributes to breakup of families
   - Prison is too lenient – not seen as a deterrent
   - Too many early releases – insufficient note taken of views and feelings of victims and their families
   - High cost of prison system – not effective use of resources

Below is a model paragraph answer — 4 marks awarded.

> Critics argue that prisons cost too much to run. The cost of putting someone in prison for a year is around £40,000, therefore, the prison system in Scotland is a massive burden on the tax payer. Critics argue the focus should be put on rehabilitating criminals, especially those who are repeat offenders. The costs of alternative sentences such as community service are much lower than sending someone to prison, and such a sentence will teach a criminal about the consequences of their actions. **6**

3. You are required to use the sources provided to draw valid conclusions, with supporting evidence.

   You should draw conclusions using the headings/bullet points in the question.

   An answer which merely repeats the source material without making judgements or conclusions will be awarded zero marks.

   For full marks three developed conclusions must be given.

   You should link information within and between sources in support of your conclusions.

   The conclusion can be placed either at the beginning or at the end after the evidence.

   Below is a model answer — awarded full marks 8/8.

   > *The rate of murders with knives*
   >
   > My first conclusion is that the rate of murders with knives is decreasing.
   >
   > This is supported by evidence from Source 2 which shows that in 2003/2004 there were 70 murders involving knives in Scotland and as the years have progressed this has decreased to a low of 49 in 2007/2008. This links in with Source 1 which states "the threat of a custodial sentence may work as the number of murders with knives has dropped since 2003/2004."
   >
   > *The reasons young people carry knives*
   >
   > The conclusion is that young people carry knives for a variety of reasons.
   >
   > Source 1 tells us that "some young people carry a knife for their own personal safety when they go out." However, Source 3 states "many youths have stated that carrying a knife is part of being in a gang and they have to be seen to be armed - peer pressure is a key factor."
   >
   > *The views on methods to reduce knife crime*
   >
   > My conclusion is that most people believe a jail sentence will reduce knife crime.
   >
   > This is supported by Source 2 where it shows that in a public opinion survey 67% of people believed an automatic jail sentence reduces knife crime and only 29% think community service or a fine (4%) was the correct method. This links with Source 1 which states "Many members of the public believe that people who carry knives should automatically be sent to jail which would reduce crime — very few people think a fine would work." Lastly my conclusion is backed up by Source 3, which states "young people have admitted that a jail sentence would make them think twice about carrying a knife." **8**

Section 3

Part E

1. Credit answers which describe government responses to social inequalities, economic inequalities or a combination of the two.

   Credit reference to aspects of the following:
   - Educational issues in your selected country
   - Any issues relating to healthcare and inequalities within your selected country
   - Issues relating to law and order within your selected country
   - Differences in housing between different groups in your selected country
   - Wealth, employment and living standards inequalities in your selected country

   Below is a model paragraph answer — 3 marks awarded.

   > The country I have studied is South Africa.
   >
   > Within education the South African Government has responded to the poor educational attainment of many of its country's young people by increasing spending on education — in 2012 it invested 21% of the entire spending on education. Students in poorer schools do not need to pay school fees. New schools have also been built and in the Western Cape only 4% of schools have no electricity. **6**

2. Credit references to the following:
   - Access to elections within your selected country
   - Level of choice and competition between political parties/candidates within your selected country
   - The extent to which freedom of speech, religion, media is allowed ie protest, Internet within your selected country
   - Political integrity and no corruption within your selected country

   Below is a model paragraph answer — 4 marks awarded.

   > The country I have studied is South Africa.
   >
   > Within South Africa opposition parties and concerned citizens such as Desmond Tutu are worried by government attempts to limit the freedom of the press and reduce people's political rights. The South African Broadcasting Corporation (SABC) is regarded as the mouthpiece of the ANC and at election time it favours the ANC. The press have until now been able to publish corruption and criminal actions by ANC leaders. However the ANC Government intend to pass a law, which makes it a crime to report on the activities of government politicians. **6**

3. You are required to evaluate a limited range of sources, detecting and explaining instances of exaggeration and/or selective use of facts, giving developed arguments.

   To achieve full marks you must show evidence that has been selected as it supports the view and show evidence that has not been selected, as it does not support the view.

   An answer that deals with only one side of the explanation, or does not use evidence from all sources will only be awarded a maximum of 6 marks.

   Below is a model answer — awarded full marks 8/8.

   > Brad Simpson is not being selective in the use of facts when he says "The President... remains popular amongst his own party". This is because according to Source 1 the President's popularity has remained

steadily between 80-90% of his own part between April 2009–August 2010. This backed up in Source 3 when it says that support from the President's own political party has changed little.

However, he is being selective when he says "The President remains popular, especially on the main issue for all ethnic groups". This statement is incorrect because on the issues of the Economy and Terrorism, the President did have the support of the majority of White, Black and Hispanic Americans. However, on the issue of health, the President did not have the support of the majority of White Americans as only 40% were in favour of his reforms. Also according to Source 1 the opposition party, which has a key demographic of Asians, has seen a fall in support for the President from 40% to below 20%.

Also, he is not being selective as Source 2 shows that in 8 of the 9 states more people agree with the view that he is doing a good job. However while about 54% in Wyoming support the President's party more people think that the President has done a bad job. **8**

Part F

1. Credit reference to aspects of the following:

    Issue — Poverty in Africa:
    - Famine — lack of food supply or ability to afford or grow crops
    - Disease — lack of nutrients, drinking contaminated water (associated illness kills thousands daily)
    - Increased death rates/infant mortality — deaths as a result of malnutrition and associated illnesses
    - Impact on education — poor attendance at school, work instead of learn
    - Impact on economy — less active work force

    Below is a model paragraph answer — 3 marks awarded.

    Poverty in Africa has many consequences for the people of the continent. The poverty experienced by citizens in many African countries is absolute poverty, with many people living below £1 per day, barely having enough to eat or drink in a day. Living in poverty makes people more susceptible to illness and disease. **6**

2. Credit reference to aspects of the following:

    Issue — Poverty in Africa:
    - A particular case study or example would be useful in this answer eg Sudan, DR Congo, Somalia, Mali etc.
    - United Nations — the work of specialised agencies UNICEF, WHO, UNESCO, FAO, WFP. Eg UNICEF: involved in helping meet the specific needs of children. Campaign in southern Africa to prevent AIDS transmission from mothers to children. Campaign to help child soldiers in Sudan
    - Charities and NGO's: Eg Oxfam, WaterAid, Christian Aid. Eg Warchild specifically focuses on helping children affected by conflict
    - African Union: increasing co-operation, promoting democracy, human rights and tackling extreme widespread conflict in the continent

    Below is a paragraph model answer — 4 marks awarded.

    International organisations work hard to help those in need in Africa. This help could be in an emergency situation such as during a famine or armed conflict. The United Nations has specialised agencies tasked with helping people in need around the world. UNICEF specifically works to help young people. In Africa

UNICEF works to provide education for those who are not attending school. UNICEF's 'Schools for Africa' programme has managed to raise the school enrolment rate in Rwanda to 95% in recent years, up from 74% in 2000. **6**

3. You are required to evaluate the sources provided to detect and explain instances of exaggeration and/or selective use of facts, giving developed answers.

    In order to achieve full marks you must include evidence that supports the view and you must include evidence that does not support the view and you must use all three sources.

    An answer which covers only one side of your explanation will be awarded a maximum of 6 marks.

    Below is a model answer — awarded full marks 8/8.

    The first reason Diane Lochrie is selective in her use of facts is when she states "it is obvious that increasing aid reduces poverty in African countries and improves education". Diane is selective as Source 3 shows us that in all of the African countries aid has been increased from 2003 to 2008 but in Source 2 it shows us that poverty has also increased in 4 of the selected countries. Only Ethiopia has seen a slight decrease in poverty levels from 50% to 37%.

    However, Diane was not being selective in stating that aid improves education as Source 2 tells us that literacy rates are increasing in most countries such as in Botswana from 80% to 84% and in Swaziland from 74% to 81%. Only in Zimbabwe has education not improved.

    However, Diane was also being selective in her use of facts when she stated "while those countries with increasing debt are unable to reduce the problem of HIV/AIDS" as Source 3 shows that the debt totals for Botswana, Lesotho, Swaziland and Zimbabwe have increased but Source 1 highlights only Botswana has shown an increase in the percentage of adults living with HIV/AIDS. The other three, have all seen a decrease in the percentage of adults living with HIV/AIDS meaning debt hasn't affected countries' efforts to reduce this problem — for example, 22.1% of adults were living with HIV/Aids in 2003 in Zimbabwe compared to only 15.3% in 2008. **8**

NATIONAL 5 MODERN STUDIES MODEL PAPER 3

Section 1

Part A

1. Credit reference to aspects of the following:
   - Leader of the Scottish Government
   - Direct policy in the Scottish Government
   - Spokesperson for the Scottish Government
   - Chairs Scottish Cabinet
   - Chooses members of the Scottish Cabinet and other government ministers
   - Leader of the biggest party in the Scottish Parliament
   - Takes part in First Minister's Question Time every week
   - Lead role in discussions with the UK Government
   - Represents Scotland in discussions with other devolved bodies and overseas
   - Focus of media attention

   Below is a model paragraph answer — 3 marks awarded.

   A power of the First Minister is commanding huge media attention. As First Minister you are seen as the figurehead of the Government and you have huge access to the media. An example of the First Minister using this power is when 2 former SNP MSPs resigned over the party's decision to remain part of NATO should independence happen. Alex Salmond called a press conference and was featured in all major newspapers the next day defending the decision. **6**

2. Credit reference to aspects of the following:

   Majority government works well:
   - Able to put policies into effect
   - Clear decisive decision-making
   - No need to compromise
   - Able to keep election promises

   Majority government does not work well:
   - Government may be too powerful and ignore other views
   - Unresponsive to wishes of electorate
   - Unwilling to compromise
   - Able to pursue extreme or unpopular policies

   Below is a model paragraph answer — 4 marks awarded.

   Some people believe majority government works well as the government will be able to carry out their policies. Like the current SNP majority government, long promised policies such as a referendum on independence or a minimum price on alcohol can be put forward by the government. This is good as parties are elected based on the promises in their manifesto so if a government has a majority then they have the right to carry out these policies. **6**

3. You are required to evaluate a limited range of sources, detecting and explaining instances of exaggeration and/or selective use of facts, giving developed arguments.

   To achieve full marks you must show evidence that has been selected as it supports the view and show evidence that has not been selected as it does not support the view.

   An answer that deals with only one side of the explanation, or does not use evidence from all sources will only be awarded a maximum of 6 marks.

   Below is a model answer — awarded full marks 8/8.

   Diana Jones is not being selective when she says "The campaign to end the tolls on the Forth and Tay Bridges had the support of the people of Scotland" as according to Source 1, NAAT lobbied political parties and persuaded the Liberal Democrats to support the scrapping of bridge tolls. This point is backed up by Source 2 as in the Dunfermline and West Fife by-election, the Liberal Democrats won by a massive two thousand majority over Labour.

   She is also not being selective as in Source 1 it states that local newspaper the Dundee Courier supported the campaign. This success is further emphasised in Source 3 which states that "tens of thousands" of the public supported the newspaper's campaign by signing petitions, a huge 10,000 people signed online polls and many displayed bumper stickers on their vehicles.

   However, Diana Jones is being selective as the campaign did not have the support of the Trade Unions. Source 1 states that the Trade Unions were concerned about the impact on their members. This is backed up by Source 2 which states that the Transport and General Workers Union was concerned over job losses and estimated that 175 of their members faced the sack. **8**

Part B

1. Credit reference to aspects of the following:
   - Leader of the UK Government
   - Direct policy in the UK Government
   - Spokesperson for the UK Government
   - Chairs UK Cabinet
   - Chooses members of the UK Cabinet and other government ministers
   - Leader of the biggest party in the UK Parliament
   - Takes part in Prime Minister's Question Time every week
   - Lead role in discussions with other governments from around the world
   - Focus of media attention

   Below is a model answer — 3 marks awarded.

   A power of the Prime Minister is commanding huge media attention. As Prime Minister you are seen as the figurehead of the Government and you have huge access to the media. An example of the Prime Minister using this power was when there was a terrorist attack in Woolwich. David Cameron called a press conference and was featured in all major newspapers the next day speaking on behalf of the Government condemning the attack. **6**

2. Credit reference to aspects of the following:

   Coalition government works well:
   - Parties work together so more cooperation and compromise
   - More voters feel represented in government
   - Unpopular and extreme policies less likely as government needs to maintain support.

   Coalition government does not work well:
   - Voters dissatisfied as voters generally do not vote for a coalition but for a single party who they wish to see form a government
   - May be unstable as parties find it difficult to work together
   - May be indecisive and unable to take radical but necessary decisions.

Below is a model answer — 4 marks awarded.

> Some people believe coalition government works well as it means that the government has to work together and cooperate with each other more. As it is important to satisfy more than one political party it means that decisions can't be dominated by one viewpoint. This means that the promises the parties made in their manifestos can be carried out and so more voters are represented in the government. For example, the Liberal Democrats forced a referendum on the voting system and the Conservatives forced a rise in tuition fees.　**6**

3. You are required to evaluate a limited range of sources, detecting and explaining instances of exaggeration and/or selective use of facts, giving developed arguments.

To achieve full marks you must show evidence that has been selected as it supports the view and show evidence that has not been selected as it does not support the view.

An answer that deals with only one side of the explanation, or does not use evidence from all sources will only be awarded a maximum of 6 marks.

Below is a model answer — awarded full marks 8/8.

> Christ Knight is not being selective in the use of facts when he says "Compulsory voting would improve democracy and would be popular with voters" as according to Source 1 supporters of compulsory voting say it will increase turnout and allow parties to concentrate on issues leading to more debate. This is backed up by Source 3 in which Brian Davidson MP says it will get more people interested in politics.
>
> However, Chris Knight is being selective in the use of facts as Source 1 claims that some people feel it would be wrong to force people to vote and it would be against British traditions. Indeed according to Source 3 forcing people to vote would lead to more spoilt ballot papers as many people simply do not trust politicians, especially young people who are least likely to vote as only 24% of 18–24 year olds are certain to vote (Source 2).
>
> In addition, he is also being selective as according to Source 1 compulsory voting is not part of UK law and it would be difficult to enforce and a waste of police and court time. Added to the fact that, in Source 3, MP Oliver Heald says there is little support to make it a criminal offence not to vote and he feels the answer is for politicians to excite the electorate.　**8**

Section 2

Part C

1. Credit reference to aspects of the following:
   - Lack of success in education
   - Low self-esteem
   - Lack of material goods
   - Overcrowded/low standard of housing
   - Poor diet
   - Ill health
   - Breakdown of family

Below is a model paragraph answer — 3 marks awarded.

> If a child is living in poverty they may suffer poorer health than other children who don't live in poverty. This can be to do with the fact that a child living in poverty may have a poor diet of cheap foods such as tinned or ready meals. With fruit and vegetables being expensive, parents can't afford to buy and feed their children healthier foods every day.　**4**

2. Credit reference to aspects of the following:

Government policies:
- Increase access to healthcare by increased spending
- Free prescriptions
- Health promotion and prevention campaigns
- Legal measures eg smoking ban/minimum alcohol pricing
- Measures restricting drink promotions

Individual actions:
- Better/more healthy diet eg more fruit and vegetables
- More exercise eg regular walking, join a gym
- Smoking — reduce or stop entirely
- Alcohol — moderate consumption
- Drugs — give up use of drugs

Below is a model paragraph answer — 4 marks awarded.

> The Government tries to improve the health of the general population in various ways. Firstly, the Government can introduce new laws that it believes will make people healthier. For example, in 2006 the Government introduced the smoking ban. This prevented people from smoking in public places such as in bars and restaurants. This has led to many people stopping smoking and fewer suffering illness through passive smoking. Due to the smoking ban, rates of cancer have fallen and the health of the population has improved.　**6**

3. You must use a limited range of sources by selecting evidence from them in order to make and justify a decision/recommendation.

You will be awarded up to three marks for a justification depending on relevance and development of the evidence.

You will be highly credited if you make justifications which show interaction between the sources.

For full marks, you must justify your decision/recommendation and explain why you have rejected the other option. Answers, which deal with only one decision, will be awarded a maximum of eight marks.

Across the whole answer you must use all 3 sources to achieve full marks.

Below is a model answer — awarded full marks 10/10.

> In my role as Scottish Government advisor I have decided to recommend Option 2, to scrap the scheme which pays smokers to stop smoking.
>
> My first reason for this is highlighted in Source 1 where is states that "many NHS staff think that other methods such as nicotine gum are more effective in helping smokers to give up cigarettes." This links in with Source 3 where Maria Logan states "alternatives such as nicotine gum and patches have proved to work in the long run."
>
> Another reason to choose Option 2 is shown in Source 2 where the percentage success rate of counselling tell us that people who have been given 91-300 minutes of counselling have a 27% success rate of stopping smoking. This links with Source 2 which states "long-term counselling has proven to be a very effective method." Source 1 also tells us that "payments will be made for a maximum of 12 weeks" with Maria Logan highlighting in Source 3 that "it is unrealistic to expect people to give up for good after only 12 weeks." This, therefore, renders the scheme pointless.

A final reason to choose Option 2 is from Source 1 which states that "some local people say it is unfair that smokers are getting extra money while others living in poverty get nothing." Maria Logan backs this up in Source 3 when she states "Many non-smoking families are living in poverty, but they are not being paid £12.50 extra a week to help with their shopping."

I did not choose Option 1, to extend the scheme which pays smokers to stop smoking across the whole of Scotland, as although Source 1 states "it is hoped 1800 smokers will sign up for the project" Source 1 also highlights that in fact "after 3 months only 360 people had signed up to the project in Dundee." The scheme, therefore, isn't popular and should be scrapped. **10**

Part D

1. Credit reference to aspects of the following:
   - Maintain law and order eg police on the beat
   - Detect crimes eg carry out investigations, interview witnesses, process evidence
   - Crime prevention eg visiting schools, Neighbourhood Watch
   - Protection of the public eg security at football matches
   - Initiatives eg knife amnesties
   - Involvement in Court System

   Below is a model paragraph answer – 3 marks awarded.

   The main role of the police is to maintain law and order in society. They do this in a variety of different ways. Firstly, the police will work on crime prevention. In doing this they will observe the public and patrol on the beat. The police will also visit schools and give presentations on issues such as drug and knife crime. Through crime prevention the rate of criminal activity is greatly reduced. **4**

2. Credit reference to aspects of the following:
   - Prison is not effective especially for short sentences
   - High level of recidivism leading to many questioning effectiveness of prison
   - Relatively few opportunities for rehabilitation
   - Prisons are expensive and overcrowded
   - Success of drug courts in rehabilitating offenders
   - Electronic tags less expensive than prison
   - Success of restorative justice especially for young offenders

   Below is a model paragraph answer – 4 marks awarded.

   Scottish courts often decide to use alternative punishments to prison. The first reason for this is that Scotland's prisons are already overcrowded. Instead of putting a criminal in jail for a short sentence, a community service punishment or a fine may be more appropriate and it solves the issue of overcrowding the prison system which in turn leads to a poor standard of living for prisoners, stress on prison staff and unwanted negative media attention on the prison service. **6**

3. You must use a limited range of sources by selecting evidence from them in order to make and justify a decision/recommendation.

   You will be awarded up to three marks for a justification depending on relevance and development of the evidence.

   You will be highly credited if you make justifications which show interaction between the sources.

For full marks, you must justify your decision/recommendation and explain why you have rejected the other option. Answers, which deal with only one decision, will be awarded a maximum of eight marks.

Across the whole answer you must use all 3 sources to achieve full marks.

Below is a model answer – awarded full marks 10/10.

In my role as government advisor I have decided to recommend Option 2 that the government should not install more CCTV cameras.

My first reason for recommending Option 2 is found in Source 1 which states "some research indicates where cameras are installed crime increases in nearby areas without CCTV cameras." This is backed up by Source 3 where Pauline Clark states "at best, CCTV only makes offenders move away from areas with cameras to commit crimes where there are none." Installing more cameras will only continue this trend.

Another reason to choose Option 2 is found in Source 3 where Pauline Clark states that "installing CCTV does not reduce crime rates." Source 1 backs this up stating "a case study in the Greater Glasgow area could find no link between the installation of CCTV cameras and a reduction in crime." Figures from source 2 proves this showing that after CCTV was installed in an inner city estate crimes actually increased by 14%. This means installing more CCTV would be pointless.

A final reason to back up my recommendation is found in Source 1 where it states that "many members of the public are concerned that more CCTV cameras means a loss of civil liberties and an invasion of privacy." This is backed up by source 2 where it shows 36% of people believed CCTV was an invasion of privacy. Pauline Clark also states in Source 3 "CCTV is an invasion of privacy as most ordinary citizens do not commit crimes but still have their movements followed and recorded up to 300 times per day." The last thing we need is more CCTV cameras following innocent people.

The reason I didn't choose Option 2 is although John Morton states "CCTV can save tax payers money by speeding up court cases" Source 1 states "Scotland's cities already have too many cameras in operation compared to other countries, costing huge amounts of money." **10**

Section 3

Part E

1. Credit reference to aspects of the following:
   - The right to vote in local and national elections
   - The right to freedom of speech in public and online
   - The right to protest
   - The responsibility to turn out and use the vote
   - The responsibility to use speech sensibly with specific reference to a G20 country's control
   - The responsibility to ensure that protests are government approved

   Below is a model paragraph answer – awarded 3 marks.

   The country I have studied is China. One right people have in China is the right to use the Internet to find out information or communicate with other. However, a responsibility is to avoid websites that are banned by the Government and to avoid discussing politics in a negative way. An example of a website which is banned in China is Facebook. **6**

2. Credit reference to aspects of the following:
   - Educational issues in your selected country
   - Any issues relating to healthcare and inequalities within your selected country
   - Issues relating to law and order within your selected country
   - Differences in housing between different groups in your selected country

Below is a model paragraph answer — 4 marks awarded.

> The country I have studied is China. In China there are inequalities between the poor rural communities and the rich urban areas. In the rural areas people have less access to well paid jobs as the work is mainly local and agricultural. Whereas in urban areas workers have access to large Chinese and multinational businesses where the wages are usually much higher. Especially in Special Economic Zones such as Hong Kong. For example, Foxconn, the company who assembles Apple products pays their workers almost double the average wage within China.   **6**

3. You are required to use the sources provided to draw valid conclusions, with supporting evidence.

You should draw conclusions using the headings/bullet points in the question.

An answer which merely repeats the source material without making judgements or conclusions will be awarded zero marks.

For full marks three developed conclusions must be given.

You should link information within and between sources in support of your conclusions.

The conclusion can be placed either at the beginning or at the end after the evidence.

Below is a model answer — awarded full marks 8/8.

HIV/AIDS in mothers and children

The conclusion is there has been good progress in the treatment of mothers and children with HIV/AIDS.

According to Source 1 the number of pregnant women on antiretroviral treatment (ART) which prevents mother to child transmission of HIV, almost doubled between 2007 and 2008. ART is now available to over 50% of those in need. In addition, the percentage of pregnant women who are HIV positive receiving ART has steadily increased since 2004 according to Source 3.

Provincial Differences

The Conclusion is that provincial differences remain in those who are dying from HIV/AIDS.

In Source 2 it shows that the number of people who die due to AIDS is much higher in some regions such as KwaZulu, whereas in other regions such as the Western Cape the number is much lower. This corresponds to the information in Source 1 which shows that as some areas have a greater number of those with HIV/AIDS, this has reduced the life expectancy in some Provinces.

How effective the Government is in dealing with HIV/AIDS

The conclusion is that the Government is taking the problem more seriously and is increasing spending to try to tackle the problem.

Source 1 states the UN report found that the South African Government's plan to tackle HIV/AIDS was one of the largest treatment programmes in the world. This corresponds with Source 3 in which the percentage of women of are HIV receiving ART has increased year on year and has risen from 15% in 2004 to 73% in 2008.   **8**

Part F

1. Credit reference to aspects of the following:

Issue — War
- Child soldiers
- Orphans
- Refugees
- Breakdown of society
- Lack of education
- Political unrest

Below is a model paragraph answer — 3 marks awarded.

> The consequences of war on the population of a country can be devastating. Children can be recruited to fight in wars as child soldiers which can lead to children being killed or killing other people. Child soldiers are treated terribly by their captors and can often be physically and mentally abused. This has happened in many African countries such as Sudan and Mali.   **4**

2. Credit reference to aspects of the following:

Issue: Poverty in Africa
- Political corruption or instability
- Debt
- Lack of infrastructure
- Armed conflict
- Trade issues
- Natural disasters — famine, floods, etc.

Below is a model paragraph answer — 4 marks awarded.

> It can be very difficult tackling poverty in Africa due to corruption in politics. Developed nations and charities may donate aid to a country in the hope that it will help the poor and suffering in that country, however, it has been the case in the past in Africa that government officials have stolen aid money or misspent it meaning the aid does not filter through to the needy. The current leader of Sudan, Omar al-Bashir, has been accused of siphoning aid money and has expelled aid agencies from the country over the years.   **6**

3. You are required to use the sources provided to draw valid conclusions, with supporting evidence.

You should draw conclusions using the headings/bullet points in the question.

An answer which merely repeats the source material without making judgements or conclusions will be awarded zero marks.

For full marks three developed conclusions must be given.

You should link information within and between sources in support of your conclusions.

The conclusion can be placed either at the beginning or at the end after the evidence.

Below is a model answer — awarded full marks 8/8.

Changes in the level of terrorist incidents worldwide

My first conclusion is that the number of terrorist related incidents has declined in recent years. Source 1 states "the number of terrorist related incidents worldwide dropping from a high in 2008 to a low in 2012." This links with Source 2 which shows that in 2008 there were 13,435 incidents and in 2012 there was only 10,138 highlighting a significant decline.

Motives behind terrorist incidents in selected countries

The conclusion is that religion is the most common cause of terrorist incidents. This is supported by evidence from Source 3 which shows political reasons are the main cause of terrorism in the USA but religion is the main cause in Afghanistan, Pakistan and Somalia with hundreds of incidents in these countries. This links in with Source 1 which states "In Afghanistan, Pakistan and Somalia the most common motive for terror was religious reasons."

The levels of terrorist incidents in selected countries

My conclusion is that the level of terrorist incidents is decreasing in some countries but increasing in others. This is supported by evidence firstly from Source 1 which states "The amount of incidents in individual countries has also come down with the amount in Afghanistan decreasing. However, the number of terrorist incidents in Somalia and Spain has increased which is a worrying trend." This links with Source 2 which shows in 2010 Afghanistan suffered 956 terrorist incidents then in 2012 suffered fewer with 912. Source 2 also shows the increase in Spain and Somalia — Spain increasing by 2 and Somalia by 49. **8**

Acknowledgements

Permission has been sought from all relevant copyright holders and Hodder Gibson is grateful for the use of the following:

Figures from the table 'Who do you think performed best overall in the party leaders' debates?' taken from www.yougov.co.uk, public domain (Model Paper 1 page 7);

The logo for G8 Canada. Reproduced with permission of the Department of Foreign Affairs, Trade and Development Canada, Ottawa 2013 (Model Paper 1 page 19);

An extract from *The Dundee Courier* about the bridge tolls campaign © D.C. Thomson & Co. Ltd Dundee Scotland (Model Paper 3 page 4).

Hodder Gibson would like to thank SQA for use of any past exam questions that may have been used in model papers, whether amended or in original form.